More Than a Game

More Than a Game

LIFE LESSONS FROM PHILADELPHIA'S SPORTS COMMUNITIES

NEW CITY COMMUNITY PRESS
Eliot Shorr-Parks • Steve Parks
www.newcitycommunitypress.com

New City Community Press
7715 Crittenden St #222
Philadelphia, PA 19118
www.newcitycommunitypress.com

ISBN (PRINT): 978-0-9840429-0-6
ISBN (ELECTRONIC): 978-0-9840429-1-3

Design by Elizabeth Parks

Cover image courtesy of Rebecca Savedow

Grass background image courtesy of Creative Commons and wwarby. Please visit http://www.flickr.com/photos/wwarby/ for more information.

Water background image courtesy of Creative Commons and Mary Vican. Please visit http://www.flickr.com/photos/26499572@N08/ for more information.

For Katie, Sadie, and Jude
E.S.P.

For my father, Clint Parks
S.P.

CONTENTS

ACKNOWLEDGEMENTS

More Than a Game began as a conversation over Chinese food, where discussions of the goal of community publishing and sports culture blended into a book idea. At the time, there was little reason to expect that athletes, amateur or professional, would take time out of their hectic lives to sit and talk with us, often for hours on end. We had little sense of how our small project might bring us into contact with individuals and organizations whose commitment to our city's youth and neighborhoods would inspire us on a daily basis. We want to begin then by thanking those athletes and organizers who appear in this book. We hope this book does justice to the impact you have made on our city.

Moving an idea from a conversation, to taped interviews, to chapters, to the book you now hold in your hands took a team in its own right. For that reason, we also want to acknowledge the student interns who supported the logistics of this project: Austin Argenti, Benjamin Klein, Danielle Mancinelli and Beth Uzwiak. Without the unwavering support of the following, we might never have met many of the individuals featured in this book: Luke Butler, Bonnie Clark, Donna Cooper, Ben Herold, Margaret Hughes, Brian Johnson, Marisol Lezcano, Mark Lyons, Adele MacDonald, Larry Needle, Ryan Nissan, Tysha Monique, Louis Antonio Ortiz, Joe Saville, Deanna Sabec, Larry Shenk, Laura Shubilla, Jacquie Thomas and Pamela Browner White. Finding the proper home for this project has also led to an important alliance with Temple University Press. So we also need to thank Micah Kleit, for his vision on how our independent press, New City Community Press, and Temple UP might work together. His insights, along with those of the Temple University Press Advisory Board, have been invaluable.

Finally, every book project is a deeply personal commitment – a faith that at the end of the day, what is produced will be of value not only to the authors, but to the readers as well. While we have worked together on this project, we want to take a moment to thank, as individuals, those who have sustained our effort:

SP: There is a cliché moment in any sports interview, where the athlete thanks his family for their unwavering support. In this case, cliché becomes reality. As always, I am deeply indebted to Lori, Sadie and Jude, for everything they add to my life. I am also grateful to close friends who have helped keep this project on track when it threatened to veer off into academic discourse or writing pedagogy (my day job) and leave behind the power of the stories being told: Brian Johnson, Jim Seitz, John Burdick and Jeff Bellamy. Finally, I want to particularly thank my youngest son's sports coaches, who without knowing it, were a guiding spirit in what I hoped to capture in this book: Matthew Grady, Patrick Fillimore and Chris Plant. My children were lucky to have them as coaches and teachers.

ESP: In my life, I have been blessed by the people around me. I want to take time to thank them all—because without them, none of this would be possible. First, I want to thank those who have read my articles or taken time to talk sports with me. To Gary Cobb, for showing me the in and outs of sports journalism. Life is not complete without good friends, and I am lucky to have a lot in my life—Leo Osterweil, Avi Rubinsky, Andrew Overton, Joe Magdovitz, Nick Powell, Isak Catic and Ariel Maidansky. Although he is more like a brother, I would like to especially acknowledge Alex Garcia—my life would not be the same without you.

If family is the team you spend your life with, then I have been blessed with a group of All-Stars. First, to my grandfathers, Clint and Joe: Although you have passed on, I thank you for making me realize how lucky we all are to have each other. I only wish you could have been here to share this with me. To my grandmothers, Lois and Carol: Thanks for making every trip to your house so special. For my brother Jude, simply put, you are the man. I can't wait to watch and see all the great things you accomplish in your life. To my sister Sadie, thanks for being the best sister a brother could ask for. To my parents, the older I get, the more I realize how lucky I am to have such wonderful, successful, supportive role models in my life every day.

Finally, Katie, having you in my life every day is the best thing to ever happen to me. You inspire me to be a better person. You mean more to me than you'll ever know.

MORE THAN A GAME:

Life Lessons from Philadelphia's Sports Communities

Rocky might be considered the penultimate Philadelphia sports movie. Telling the story of a working-class boxer from South Philly who, through hard work and good fortune, manages to obtain the world title, *Rocky* has been adopted by the city for its ability to express the daily struggles of Philly's many residents. Indeed, for many, the essence of Philadelphia sports is captured in *Rocky*; it is the emotional framework through which much of our city's modern sports history is framed and articulated. Not only has "Win, Rocky, Win" become the battle cry for our professional and amateur sports teams alike, but every day hundreds of residents and tourists reenact Rocky's run up the Philadelphia Arts Museum steps, bouncing up and down upon their arrival at the top, their clenched fists reaching up into the air. Moments later they head over to the Rocky statue, nestled in a shaded area off to the side, completing a modern sports pilgrimage.

More Than a Game also tells a Philadelphia sports story. In the following pages, you will read about individuals who struggled against great odds to win titles, achieve success. Memorable lines also are spoken by these individuals; aphorisms that will inspire and compel you to strive harder in your daily life. This is not, however, a book framed around the *Rocky* narrative—the lone individual who, given a unique opportunity at success, steps into his moment and succeeds. For while this is a classic American myth, it is not, we believe, an accurate description of how sports operate in Philadelphia; it does not recognize and respect the ways in which Philadelphia residents have used high school teams, community sports leagues, or professional franchises to foster a greater sense of opportunity and community across the city. It does not place individual success within community support.

For ultimately what *Rocky* gets wrong isn't that life-changing opportunities emerge from sports. It is wrong in presenting such opportunities as only possible through random luck. While such stories might *possibly* be useful in explaining one element or aspect of our city's sports culture, ultimately they necessarily fail to capture the complexity, diversity and richness of how sports operate in our city on a daily level, in the lives of residents who course about their neighborhoods every day committed to fostering and capturing the potential of a place they call home. If you look closely, you will see that while these efforts are embedded in sports, these efforts are really about mentoring, education and community building. This insight is only possible, however, if you step outside mass-produced visions of our sports culture.

We believe that to many young adults in our city, sports are a portal to a cohesive and supportive sense of community, a vital resource within urban neighborhoods that are often under tremendous stress. The work of high school and community league coaches and athletes offers a public space where communal values of hard work, team goals and achievable success are enacted daily—at every practice and in every game. At a moment when publicly-funded institutions, such as non-profit community organizations, are suffering under the "great recession," sports leagues offer a low-cost consistent presence and resource to young adults, the very individuals who are often pulled towards behaviors that are not in their immediate or long-term best interests. In these situations, the coach, the team, the league offers a haven in which new identities and opportunities for leadership can be tested, tried on and assumed as a vital element of their own being. In this way, sports serves as a vehicle through which a set of values can be inculcated, internalized and enacted. If we take such a view, we can come to understand that the sporting community is a network of individuals, teams, and organizations which fosters a sense of purpose for our youth, a network that stitches together a diverse and multilingual community within our city and moves it towards a collective purpose.

Indeed to fully understand our city's sports culture, we also need to reconfigure our sense of the "fan community." Too often, Philadelphia fans are characterized by singular moments that have turned into metonyms for an entire city's behavior—throwing snowballs at Santa

Claus, booing an injured Michael Irvin. If you listen to the fans and professional athletes, however, a more complex and rich relationship is demonstrated. Particularly when talking to members of Philadelphia's working class, it becomes clear that the push and pull between fan and player is an extended discussion over the importance of working-class values, an effort to ensure that our teams live up to the city's reputation for hard work and no excuses. It is also a conversation about different elements of the city expecting to be represented on the professional playing field, of franchises needing to see themselves not as businesses, but as neighbors. It is this image, this goal, which leads parents to take their children to games, that leads children to don the shirts of a Bobby Clarke or Carlos Ruiz. Rather than the simplistic vision of fan culture as "tailgating," then, we hope to explore how other elements of fandom help to create a concentric vision of community, moving from the immediacy of family outward to community leagues, and ultimately pointing toward the actions of professional franchises which circulate across the country.

To represent this community, we consciously decided not to frame our work as a traditional scholarly project—chapters written in academic discourse, footnotes indicating research trends and insights. Instead, we wanted to create a project that allowed residents, coaches and athletes to speak in their own terms about the ways in which participation in a sports team or program enriched their own lives and the life of their community. Indeed, what you will read in this book will be their words, as spoken by them, with little or no editorial changes. In choosing who to speak to for this project, our general intent—with some exceptions—was to interview individuals who had emerged from a working-class background and went on to become active in Philadelphia's sports community—either as athlete or coach. We were also interested in individuals who could speak to how their participation in sports translated into other areas of their life—whether personal or professional. Where individuals helped to create or were active in a sports league, we were interested in their thoughts on how the league impacted the community in which it existed. Throughout, we were committed to trying to represent the diversity of heritages and backgrounds that make up our city.

We believe important and compelling stories have emerged from these efforts, stories that can be used to teach and inform both the current and future participants in Philadelphia sports about the values and goals of its sports community. As you read through this book, you will hear:

Jordan Berman and Frank Greco talk about the rich history of street games, such as half ball and hose ball, which were the first games many working class children played "back in the day" on Philadelphia streets;

Angelo Cataldi, Vanessa Rodriguez and Nick Bradley demonstrate the importance of fathers in shaping the values they bring to their understanding of sports and community;

Bobby Clarke, Chris Pronger and Leonard Weaver talk about how working class values learned from their parents provided them an insight into the values of sports that carried into their playing careers;

Rob Enslin discusses the importance of the "Broad Street Bullies" as he navigated a simultaneously supportive and difficult childhood and Dave Leonardi speaks to how a commitment to the Flyers has enriched his life;

Danny Diaz share moments where his teenage years seemed to be heading off track, an experience that led him to create a youth football league in Kensington. Other sports leagues directors, such as Dan Winterstein of Mt. Airy Baseball, build off Diaz's story to talk about the role of sports in building local community;

Leroy Johnson reminisce about growing up in Philadelphia in the 1920's, watching Jack Johnson, the first African-American World Champion, spar in South Philadelphia, then face racial discrimination when he tried to swim in public pools. Alyson Goodner then "flips the script" by discussing how swimming on an integrated recreation team impacted her life;

Rami Ibrahim tell how a commitment to sports helped him overcome discrimination after his family moved to Philadelphia during the first Gulf War, providing him with a work ethic that enabled him to become the first Palestinian World Muy Thai Champion;

Bill Giles and Joe Banner talk about the role of their franchises in representing and supporting the diverse backgrounds and needs of Philadelphia's neighborhoods. Tina Sloan Green builds off their stories, showing how her commitment to African-American women athletes grows out of her own history and commitment to equity;

Carlos Ruiz and Rubén Amaro, Jr., remind us of the importance of the Latino community in developing a vibrant and engaged sense of sports in Philadelphia;

Sonny Hill share how his childhood helped to inform the creation and success of the Sonny Hill League, an effort to infuse a basketball league with the idea that "Education is Your Best Shot." A story echoed in the life history of former Eagle, Gary Cobb;

Michael Nutter, Herman Douglas and Ed Rendell speak to how their sports experiences led to their later successes and commitment to education, community and Philadelphia;

Finally, Larry Colangelo offers a final reminder to the reader of the sheer joy victory can bring to a fan, a fan-base, and a city.

We hope that taken collectively, these stories present an intimate portrait of the role of sports in Philadelphia, from the personal lives of our neighbors and friends to the role of professional franchises in our city. And while there will necessarily be overlap in themes between chapters, we have structured the book to move the reader from a sense of Philadelphia's sporting past, through the role of mentors in instilling important values about work and respect in children. The chapters then follow the path of young adults as they move onto and struggle to achieve on advanced sports teams, ultimately bringing a commitment to sports into their adult lives as coaches, commissioners and fans. The book culminates in a reminder of how victories in sports are often the result of all these moments combined by focusing on the 2008 World Series victory of the Philadelphia Phillies.

Of course, we can hardly claim to capture all the stories of Philadelphia sports. There are certainly athletes, teams and leagues that would have been welcomed additions. Absences are a necessary element in any anthology of this type. At those moments, we take comfort in the advice given by a community publisher from the United Kingdom who once told us, "You can't possibly capture everyone's story, but you must capture stories that speak to the community as a whole." We have tried to meet that challenge by finding experiences that speak to the broad and basic values of the sports community. If as you read this book, you find yourself asking why a certain person isn't included, our hope is that his or her name occurs to you because the collection has given you a new way to consider this person or team. Hopefully, such moments can be used to initiate a discussion with a student, colleague or friend on the true meaning of sports in Philadelphia.

For ultimately, we hope *More Than a Game* can lead to sports in our city being seen as a vital site of literacy instruction. Typically, when sports and literacy are connected, what is meant is the ability of sports statistics to teach math; of sports history to teach about civil rights progress. We do not deny such benefits. We would argue, however, that sports offer a unique combination of intellectual and pragmatic literacy skills. For the young adult who plays a sport, he is learning how to study a skill, how practice perfects that skill and how such skills are useful only when placed in terms of a collective team goal. As he then moves on to manage a team, he is not just learning the game, but learning how to teach values, organize projects, set goals and achieve collective results. For those who then remain active by organizing leagues, they are not just organizing a sport, but learning how to find resources, schedule events, build community support and participation. All of these lessons are learned within the enriched paradigm of valuing the local community and the future of the next generation of city residents. In effect, sports teach individuals how to build *community*.

We did not always have this insight. After almost two years into this project, we had the opportunity to visit with Sonny Hill of the Sonny Hill League. At that point in our work, we had a series of powerful stories, but perhaps not yet an understanding of what we had found. Sitting on the bleachers at Audenried High School, Mr. Hill asked, "Do you see what is happening here?" I looked at the game. "No," he said, and gestured to the stands, full of parents and children, cheering the good play of each team. He pointed to volunteer coaches, mentoring young adults in the skills that would aid them in their future goals. He pointed to referees, guiding players through the technicalities of the game. He was, I realized, asking us to see the community that sports can create, to understand the value of such moments and to seek to articulate those values for the readers of this book. He was asking us to see that it was about more than a scoreboard; it was about more than a basketball game.

At its best, our book is an attempt to listen and learn from those who have spent their lives in gyms, on playing fields and at hockey rinks; individuals who through their coaching or life experiences have drawn forth the collective best from our city's youth. Ultimately, it is an attempt to share those lessons with others.

Rather than asking someone to emulate the individual achievements of a movie hero's run up a set of steps, we are hoping this collection of stories will inspire you to stand on the sidelines and take part in the difficult and inspiring work that marks sports in Philadelphia.

For ultimately, we believe anyone who has attended an Eagles game, cheered on the Flyers, or paraded down Broad Street with the Phillies, understands there is something more to sports in Philadelphia. It's more then just three periods or nine innings. It's more then a first down.

Sports have always stood for more. It's playing with your friends. It's watching your parents cheer you in the stands. It's giving your son the glove you played with. It's not letting down your teammates. It's digging deeper. It's trying harder. It's teamwork. It's winning. It's losing. It's learning from both.

Sport's is a lot of things. But it's not just a game.

It's *More Than A Game*.

MICHAEL NUTTER

"The Philly fan wants you to put yourself out there. Understanding that, yeah, you might get smacked by a line backer, but that is your job. And whether you catch the ball or not, it's about effort. Philadelphia fans want to see the effort."

Philadelphia is a city of great history, culture, art and education. It's a real place.

Philadelphia is truly one of the great cities of the world. It's an international city. It's a port city. It's a river city. It's the center of commerce and industry. It's a city where people are passionate about issues and ideas. They care. People in Philadelphia actually give a damn about things. And that's part of who we are and what we are about. It's part of what makes Philadelphia such a great town.

I'm proud to say I grew up here. I was raised in West Philadelphia, 55th and Larchwood. The neighborhood today is the same as it was back then. It's a middle class neighborhood. While all our parents worked, most had not gone to college. However, almost everybody on the block in my cohort of friends went to college or had opportunities to go to college. Often, we were the first in our families to go to college. So it was very much a working class community, full of serious people who cared about their kids. It had a great sense of community.

Growing up, like most kids in the city, I played sports all the time. I played football, baseball and basketball. I also played stickball, step ball, dodge ball, king block. I even played marbles from time to time. I also went to Franklin Field with my father when the Eagles played there or to the Spectrum when the Sixers played there. But the sport my father and I followed the most was boxing. I saw Kenny Briscoe, William Monroe, Bobby "Boogaloo" Watts. I saw some great fights as a kid. It was an incredible era of Philadelphia fighters.

Politics is a lot like sports, there is no question about it. Politics may not be as well-regulated as sports, but there is certainly a competitiveness to it, a certain amount of mental, physical, spiritual training to it. It has a certain ebb and flow, and at the end there is victory. I fell into politics to some extent. I met a lot of political people when I was working at the Impulse nightclub in North Philly, so I started coming to City Council meetings. I was in my twenties at this point. My life-long ambition growing up was to be a doctor—I wanted to help people. With my job now, though, I get to do that as well.

I've been lucky to be the mayor of a city that values sports as much as Philadelphia does.

Sports, whatever your sport, organized leagues or pick-up, are an important component of life. Leagues like the Sonny Hill League and Police Athletic League are important parts of the community. It's not about whether you are going to be a basketball star, football star, tennis star or hockey star. It really is more about the engagement, the interaction. Learning about self-discipline, teamwork, getting along with other people; even if you are star, you learn how to support your fellow teammates. You learn what sportsmanship is all about.

So I think there are many life lessons learned that have nothing to do with the mechanics of the sport. It's really about showing up every day, being prepared, being dedicated and understanding that you are part of something larger than just yourself. I learned a great deal from sport. I still have great friends from when I played in high school. I am sure the same continues for folks who go on to play in college.

There is also something about Philadelphians and sports. Mike Schmidt had just an incredible quote that I have used from time to time: "Philadelphia is a place where you can experience the thrill of victory, and the agony of reading about it the next day." This is a very passionate town. Everybody's got something to say, everybody's got an opinion. And the next person knows more than the last person—the player should have done this, could have done that, what about this.

The Philly fan wants you to put yourself out there. Understanding that, yeah, you might get smacked by a linebacker, but that is your job. And whether you catch the ball or not, it's about effort. Philadelphia fans want to see the effort. This is a hard working kind of town, people take their jobs seriously. They want their sports stars to do the same thing. No matter how big a star you are in the town, the Philly fan never wants our stars to get too far above the fans. So if you, as a sports star, start thinking that the game is about you and not about the fans, you are going to have a problem right here in this town. We don't suffer the prima donnas easily.

Sports, I think, at least in this town, is also often a barometer of how people are feeling. At least during football season, on any Monday you can pretty much tell by the first 15 minutes of conversation with co-workers whether or not the Eagles won the day before. Baseball is everyday, so it's up, down, you know. And it definitely has an effect on the mood of the city.

That's what made the Phillies Championship in 2008 so special. As the Phillies were going through the playoffs that year, we are in the midst of one of the worst recessions this city had ever seen. But people were upbeat, they were nice, they were excited. There was electricity in the stadium that was somewhat indescribable. There was just this sense that we were going to win this game. Our last baseball championship was the 1980's World Series. And so it had been a long time and we had been watching this team of great promise and they had been building for some time, and it was a most incredible feeling when they won. I had never personally experienced something like that before. I saw the win in 1980 on TV, but I was not at the game. So to be in the new ballpark, seeing this great team, knowing the struggles that they had been through in '08, it was an amazing experience. And whether you follow the sport or not, you kind of get caught up in it. It's an incredible feeling for an individual and for the city.

So sports is about community. It's about something you don't do by yourself. There is at least a person that has to work with you. It's getting along with large groups of people, it's about dedication and commitment, it's about showing up every day, it's about the proper mental attitude, it's about how you interact with people who are focused on a particular goal to try and accomplish something. So sports teaches you about life, whether you use those lessons in a game or to run a city government. It's that sense of camaraderie that football coaches talk about: "It's about the team." And no matter the context, we still need to execute. We still need to take care of the fundamentals. Philadelphia is our team, and we are all trying to move in the same direction.

LEROY JOHNSON

"I couldn't get in the pool. They felt I would 'pollute' the water."

I was three years old when my father moved my family to Philadelphia in 1917. I've lived here ever since, 94 years.

I can remember seeing Jack Johnson at an exhibition for the Wild Bill Hickok Show on the Southwest corner of 17th and South Street, right next to Waxman's shop. I was a 10 or 12 year-old boy. He was an internationally-known black boxer. You can't imagine how excited we were. I got a big kick out of it. When I was older, I went to see Joe Louis and Billy Conn fight in New York. I got the tickets through a numbers runner.

I also remember there was a colored team in Philadelphia, The Hilldale Athletics Club, played in the Eastern Colored League. They played at 44th and Parkside. It was a scrub stadium. Not much of a stadium at all, but it was a ballpark. The Negro Baseball League had some darn good players, like Satchel Paige, as good as any player in the National League, but they never got national attention. My father was quite a good baseball player when he was a young man in the south. Of course, those games were all colored, no integration whatsoever, but my mother told me he could hit a ball a country mile. When he moved north that all went out the window because there was no opportunity unless he played semi-pro ball. As a sports activity, that was out of the picture for him. So he opened a barbershop.

He was considered one of the better barbers, though, so some of the Negro League players use to come in there. I got to know quite a few players on a more or less personal basis. Mostly, they were "regular Joes," real nice guys. A couple of them had their ass up on their shoulders, but not so many. Most of the guys were pretty regular. They did anything from sweeping the floor to hanging wallpaper during the

off-season, but during the baseball season they played baseball. They were well respected. They were no heroes or anything. But they were respected.

My sport was swimming, but the 52nd St. YMCA was the only place you could swim at that time if you were colored. Even then I had to be a member of the Overbrook High School swim team. So I made the team. Our first meet was at the Girard College swimming pool. Now they wouldn't even let me in the door, wouldn't even let me in the gate. Stephen Girard had put in his will that no coloreds and no Indians could use it. That was before Cecil B. Moore went to the Pennsylvania Supreme Court and broke Girard's will. So I wasn't allowed to swim.

But the team went on into the pool. They weren't not going to swim because of me. No. No. That didn't mean anything to them. I was lucky to be able to swim at the YMCA. That's the way they felt. I don't think anyone in that group was super conscious. Track meets were perfectly all right being integrated, but the swimming team had difficulty. As long as we swam at Southwest Y at 52nd and Samson, it was all right for colored students to swim. But a lot of other schools, I couldn't get in the pool. They felt I would "pollute" the water.

I did have a different swimming experience, however. When I graduated from Overbrook High School in 1931, there were no jobs because of the Depression. When I was going to high school, unless you were a professional, as a Negro, all you could get were menial jobs. If you were a professional, of course, that was a different story. You could get a job as a porter in a store. Or if it were a small "mom and pop" store, you would be more or less part of the family. There you were a clerk in the store, but you cooked, cleaned, stocked, you did everything. In your larger well-established organizations, if you were Negro, you were relegated to the menial jobs.

So I became an apprentice barber. I wasn't making any money, though. Then along came Roosevelt's Civilian Conservation Corps. At that time, your family had to be on relief to get in there. Well, my family wasn't on relief, but I wasn't making money to speak of. So I made a deal with the family across the street. They would sponsor me as a member of their family. I would get a dollar a day. They would get a similar sum. They were supposed to split this money with my family.

My group was sent up into northwest Pennsylvania to clear out forested areas. When we were finished, it was almost like a park, a forested park. Of course, our work team was segregated. The head was a retired army officer, a white sergeant, on leave. The rest of the group was all colored. Well, one time during my free time, I discovered a creek that was pretty deep—six, seven feet deep in spots. I was still a good swimmer, even then. Once while I was swimming, there were local white kids swimming too. It was the first time I ever saw them. I was on a tree limb six feet away, and I did a jackknife off the tree limb. These kids started clapping. We became quite friendly. They even took me to their homes. I was a novelty up in that area. Most of those people had never seen a Negro. I remember I left at the end of five months, but I really enjoyed that swimming hole.

Today skin color doesn't amount to much. For today's athletes, whether they are in school or in the professional leagues, it's a whole new ballgame. They're just players for the most part. Good or bad, their race is not considered a prime factor. No one group thinks it's any better than the other one. I guess somebody decided it's time to stop being stupid.

ome

ors

JORDAN BERMAN

"It cost a quarter to get in, maybe cheaper. You would go buy a ticket and watch the game."

I grew up in West Philly – all over it. From 1945 to 1948, my parents lived in six different locations. Quite often there were two to four families living together. All those families and only one bathroom. Some families would even have to move at night. It was cheaper to move than to pay back rent, so folks would move all around the neighborhood. We were a better off. In 1948, my parents bought their first home, 1326 Kimberly Drive, Overbrook Park. The house cost us $7,800 dollars. It wasn't much, but for the first time, it was ours.

Times were different from today. We always had clothes to wear and food to eat, but sports equipment fell into another category. My friends and I didn't play sports with purchased equipment. Gloves, bats, and balls were just not in the budget. So we would play football by folding newspapers and wrapping them in tape. We made baseballs by wrapping electrical tape around any small hard object we could find. The only purchased item was a pinky ball, which was a little smaller than a tennis ball and made of imitation rubber. It cost a nickel. We used it to play stoop ball, box ball, and chink. When it lost its air, we would cut it in half and play half ball. On days when there were no pinky balls or half balls, we would play hose ball. Hose ball is played with a hunk of hose about 3-4 inches long and a broom stick. The pitcher would toss the hose ball, and the batter would hit it as hard as he could with a broomstick. If you hit it far enough, it was home run. When we weren't playing ball, we were listening to baseball games on the radio. Home games were aired live from the stadium and away games came via ticker tape or telegraph.

Every once in a while I could save enough coins to take two trolleys from West Philadelphia to Shibe Park at 20th and Lehigh to watch the Philadelphia Athletics. The A's were a poorly run last place team. It

cost a quarter to get in, maybe cheaper. You would go buy a ticket and watch the game, but no one was ever there. A large crowd was a few thousand people. The A's two stars were Centerfielder Sam Chapman and side arm pitcher Russ Christopher, but by going to their games, I was lucky enough to see some of the biggest stars of the American League, such as Joe DiMaggio, Ted Williams, and Bob Feller. Sundays would feature double headers, but if the second game ran late, it was stopped because the city's Blue Laws prevented sports after 6pm.

In my junior year at Overbrook High School, I tried out for and made the Junior Varsity basketball team. I never played in a game because I had an after school job. At that time, Overbrook was a hotbed for basketball. Jackie Moore and Hal Lear were stars, and in my Senior Year, Wilt Chamberlain arrived as a 6'9" freshman. He towered over all the competitors. His nickname was "Dippy" because he sort of dipped the ball in the basket. It was a rude awakening to my understanding of sports when five little guys from West Catholic beat Overbrook in the 1954 City Championship.

I went to work right after high school and married ten days before my 19th birthday. When I was twenty-one, my wife gave birth to our first son. When he was eight years old, he and I started to go to all the Eagles games. A couple of years later, his younger brother joined us. The Vet was not yet built so the home games were played at Franklin Field. I was at the Eagles NFL Championship victory in 1960 when Chuck Bednarick stopped the Packers Jim Taylor in the final seconds to help the Eagles win 17-13.

My four sons were sports fans as youngsters, but today, their families, business careers, and other interests have taken over. Fortunately for me, sports are very important to most of my fifteen grandchildren. We share season tickets to the Sixers and Flyers games and our grandchildren regularly attend the Phillies and the Eagles.

I use football to teach them math. I say to them, if a team scores three touchdowns, misses an extra point, kicks a field goal, then gets a safety, how many points do they have? At a very young age, they would be able to pop out answers. But the real joy to me is that on most Sunday afternoons throughout the football season, at least two and sometime as many as eight grandchildren are at my house trying to root the Eagles in. We talk about many things, such as character or lack of it, and I do believe that their present day mathematical skills were honed to perfection in some of those long ago Sunday afternoons.

Hopefully, I've been able to teach them life lessons during these very enjoyable times. I've told you what I've remembered, not necessarily the truth.

TINA SLOAN GREEN

"Talent has no color."

I grew up, until I was 14 years old, in Eastwick, Philadelphia. It was the country in the city. Talking about fresh fruits and vegetables, most families had gardens, fruit trees, grape arbors and chickens in our backyards. There were two parents in most households and such a sense of neighborhood. It was fun. Everybody knew each other. We would go out after a big storm, and if a tree had fallen down, we'd sit on the trunk and that would be our meeting spot for the block. We would play kickball, tag, wall ball, blocks and jump rope. It was just a great, fun environment.

My father worked for the Navy Yard as an electrician. My mother stayed at home, as did most mothers in that era in my neighborhood. They were home to make us our lunches because no lunches were served at the schools. We'd run home from school, eat our lunch, then we would run back. We had sandwiches and fruits. We had fresh donuts. My mother made some great soup. We had stews and greens—all those things that now, when you think of them, are delicacies. The greens were fresh because they came from my neighbor's garden. Neighbors would share goods and services. I would babysit my neighbor's granddaughter and in return our neighbor gave us fresh vegetables. So it was a neat experience.

I was one of three people in my neighborhood who went to Girls High, which was huge. Eastwick was a very small community. There were only thirteen people in my 8th grade graduating class. So it was really a dramatic change going to Girls High. Here I was involved with these brilliant girls who went to schools where they changed classes and had algebra and trigonometry and stuff. I was bright. I did pass the GHS entrance test, but I was overwhelmed in regards to changing classes and understanding the fundamentals of advanced math, science, and English. What saved me was the fact that one of the coaches, Jane Weitzenhoffer, asked me to come out for field hockey.

I had never played any organized sports, besides a May Day class competition in elementary school, but Ms. Weitzenhoffer recognized early on that I was fast and athletic. She told me to come out for the field hockey team. Back in the day, when the teacher told you to do something, you did it. So I did join the team and discovered that I was really good. The next thing you know I'm playing basketball, volleyball and softball. Plus we had a student athletic board. We'd congregate in the Athletics office before and after school and get help with our homework. Ms. Weitzenhoffer was also really good about nurturing the needy students. I guess she realized that there were only a few African American girls in the entire school, so she gave some of us the academic and emotional support that we needed to survive in this environment. I probably would have transferred if I hadn't found a comfortable home in the athletic office.

Still, I think it wasn't so much being an African American student. For me, that wasn't a big issue. My issue was mainly academics. There were these very smart girls in classes. Judith Rodin, future President of the University of Pennsylvania, was in my homeroom. I was so far behind. I thought I was smart and then I got to GHS and (laughing) find I'm just an average Joe. So sports helped me find my comfort level. Girls High did well in sports like field hockey, basketball, softball and volleyball, and I was a standout. I felt good about myself in that arena, the athletic arena, and consequently I began to catch up in my academic courses.

Ms. Weitzenhoffer did so much for me. She cared about us. She took an interest in us. She had a passion for each sport that she coached. She had a genuine interest in the well being of each young lady on the team. She cared about us on and off of the field. If we had a late match, she made sure that she drove us to the bus stop and we were safe. She's the one who pulled many of us up, helped us survive and in time excel.

After graduating from high school, I wanted to be a physical education teacher. My p.e. teachers were role models for me. My parents didn't go to college, so Ms. Weitzenhoffer told me which college would be the best for me and mapped out my career plan. She recommended West Chester because at that particular time Temple was de-emphasizing physical education. Temple didn't want to be a physical education school; it wanted to be a research institution. West Chester was more of a teacher education school.

I went out for the field hockey team at West Chester. At my first practice, my coach put us in two lines; the first line was for any of the girls who were from the Main Line; the second line was for girls who were from the city, Chester or wherever. The Main Line side became the first or second team; the other side became the third and fourth team. This was the way the coach saw it. Ironically, some days the third and fourth teams would beat the first and second teams. Fortunately for us, Vonnie Gros, who was one of the most fantastic athletes in that era in both field hockey and lacrosse, became the head coach for both sports. She was all about talent. When she recognized the talent that existed on the third and fourth teams, many third and fourth team players (including me) became starters on the first and second teams.

It was Vonnie Gros who invited me to come out for the lacrosse team. I never played lacrosse, but she was looking for talented athletes. I made varsity my first year on the team. I played defense, but I hated defense. I was an offensive player. To show how naive and bold I was, I actually went up to Vonnie one day and said, "Miss Gros, I don't think I'm in the right position, I think I'm an offensive player. Can I try offense? Can I try being a wing?" So she allowed me to try it, and I was good. I played like the guys, very little cradling with the stick. I ran with the ball, and I had a real quick wrist type shot. I was able to score.

I realized that I had the chance and the ability to be an All American in my junior year. When I was named an All American, I was exposed to club and college lacrosse team players across the area. Then, in 1969, I actually traveled with these women who I either played against or with to the World Cup in Japan. I was now playing on this tremendous team and for my country. This was Japan's first World Cup, and we were actually able to teach them the game. We did okay, losing to England which was the team to beat. I think we beat Australia.

Vonnie Gros was only one of the many strong women teachers/ coaches at West Chester. Mimi Greenwood was my badminton coach. She was very instrumental in championing me and other athletes who were sometimes overlooked. Eleanor Taylor taught officiating. She was such a strong advocate for women's sports. She was also one of the leading politicians in West Chester, a state representative. I think what I learned from Eleanor Taylor was to be a champion for your cause and not back down.

So at West Chester, we had a core of females who were strong advocates; who stood up for what they believed. Being taught by these strong women really shaped my thinking. You interacted daily with these tremendous role models who were teachers, coaches, advocates and/or politicians. You couldn't help but absorb some of their spunk. The passion they had for their sports and subject matter became a part of you.

Initially my goal after college was to coach at a public high school in Philadelphia. I wanted to make sure that more inner-city kids had the same opportunities that I had. But West Chester didn't allow students to student teach in Philadelphia, so I student-taught at Nether Providence and Indian Lane, both very elite suburban schools. When I began the process of applying for jobs, Unionville High was looking to integrate its staff. They had no African American teachers on its staff. I was hand-picked to integrate the whole school, and I was given the opportunity to start a lacrosse team and to assist with the field hockey team. They were accepting of me. There were very few if any African Americans living in the Unionville and Chadds Ford communities. I think the timing of my appointment was key. Since historically, they didn't have passionate, serious coaches, students and parents were excited about the fact that I was going to be there and I was going to coach. I brought youth and enthusiasm to the sports teams.

My second year at the school, Martin Luther King, Jr., came to the Philadelphia area. He had just spoken at Unionville High a couple months before his death. His death really touched me. His death seemed to wipe away my fears about my future direction. I felt this tremendous need to move back home to the city and really make a difference. I decided that I was going to teach in the city. By that time Jane had taken on the role as chair of a department at William Penn High School. So I rented an apartment and moved to west Philly. I felt comfortable at the new school. Jane was so good, and Lurline Jones and other very dedicated and experienced teachers were also there. It was great to have such support.

I was there for two years before going to Lincoln University. A Delta sorority sister told me that Lincoln was looking for a p.e. teacher. She called the current teacher and recommended me so I applied. Lo and behold, I got the job. I was preparing to go to Australia at the time to tour for U.S. Lacrosse, which I continued to play for until 1972. The Lincoln administration was so excited about my coming that they told me, "Don't worry if you're not back by October, the job will be waiting for you."

Lincoln was a stark contrast to what I'd been exposed to. It was an introduction to Afro-centrism. I enjoyed every moment at Lincoln. The experience grounded me, gave me a sense of identity and helped me explore my roots. There was so much history and culture at Lincoln. The students were bright and they wanted to learn. The professors were also patient and caring. I admired the extraordinary professors and coaches, such as Jean White, Floyd Laisure, Mr. Gardner and Mr. Rivera. Mr. Rivera was an outstanding badminton player. We played badminton every day. Faculty and staff did a lot of social stuff together. I felt I was part of the Lincoln family. I started a lacrosse team there. I convinced my basketball players to play lacrosse. We were terrible, but Vonnie, my old coach from West Chester, was nice enough to have her fourth team come over to play us.

I finally left Lincoln. A notice came across my desk about a new position at Temple. I said, "I'm a lacrosse coach and I'm playing with basketball players. This needs to change if I want to reach the top." Plus the salary was $11,000 a year. I was only making about $7,500. I said, "Wow this job looks like it was written for me." So I applied, went in for an interview, and, lo and behold, I was hired. I'd be going back home. I really believed that my relocation was "divine intervention." I was being called home to make a difference in my community.

Much to my surprise, when I arrived at Temple, I had to go to the campus sororities and clubs to recruit women to play. The passage of Title IX made the difference in the sport of lacrosse and field hockey. Temple was obligated to award our first scholarship, an incentive which helped recruit both parents and students. I divided it into two or three pieces to begin to get good players. So in 1978, we started to be competitive. What eventually made us good was the recruitment of talented student athletes, putting the talent in the right positions and teaching and motivating players. I recruited talented athletes from Boyertown, Ridley Park, Essington—areas where mainstream universities wouldn't be recruiting. Also my assistant coaches were excellent. Gwen Cheeseman Alexander, who eventually became one of the most celebrated goalkeepers in Olympic field hockey, was my assistant, as well as Sue Stahl, who eventually became the successful U.S. lacrosse/World Cup coach for several years.

Eventually, we began to win national championships. My 1988 team was my greatest team. It was unbelievable because we had a perfect season. The year before, that same team lost in the finals. They had to wait another year to seek revenge. This was the culminating year for a hungry team. Not only did we have a perfect season, beating all the national powerhouses, we also beat the Australian team advertised as the best team in the world. This was a thrilling win on our home field.

I wanted to stop coaching when I was on top. I wanted to leave when the university was feeling good about me and I was feeling good about the university. Plus my husband had been a huge supporter. It's very difficult to coach on an elite level without a supportive spouse. I wanted to support my children with everything, which you can't do—you can't do it all. So he would pick up the kids and take them to tennis. He had to prepare meals, check homework many days. I really think kids need you more when they're older, so that's also why I decided to quit coaching, spend more time with them and let my husband pursue his own dreams. So after I won that championship, I quit coaching.

Soon after quitting, in 1992, I began more extensive work with the Black Women in Sport Foundation (BWSF). The foundation actually started unofficially around 1974, when I first came to Temple. During the Kathy Rush era of Immaculata basketball, she held many conferences on women in sports, but we'd never see people that looked like us. Folks were never really concerned about our issues. There would never be panels with African Americans. So we decided to start our own foundation. The first Black Women's Coaches Conference was held as a continuation course at Temple. When I retired from coaching in 1992 and had the time to really devote to the foundation, I became more involved as President and Executive Director.

The issues past and present are a lack of recognition, a lack of respect, a lack of resources and marginalization. I remember when a recruiting brochure was produced at Temple featuring myself and several other black coaches. When the administrators saw the publication it was destroyed. Why? There were too many black coaches, staff and athletes featured. They said they did not want Temple to be perceived as a black school. This scenario was indicative of society at that time. It was my hope then and now that the foundation can increase opportunities for African American women in all aspects of sport, especially non traditional sports. I know that given the opportunity, African American girls could well become athletic directors or coaches or journalists or professional basketball players if they so choose. I'm so fortunate that I was able to have the opportunity.

I guess my greatest legacy would be the fact that we made a difference in these "preppy" type sports. Talent has no color. There's so much raw talent, especially in our African American community, that is untapped. I sometimes think that it's not the kids so much as the adults that interfere with developing that talent, interfere with enhancing that talent. Currently I feel encouraged because we (BWSF) and many of my former players and students during my lifetime have made a dent in the glass ceiling.

DAVE LEONARDI

"Somewhere in the late 50's, there was an NHL game on TV, and I was just mesmerized."

I played sports as far back as I can remember. I grew up in a row house in Camden, NJ. There were about 12 houses in a row, then a small space, and then another 20 houses or so. After dinner all the kids would come outside and play stick ball, half ball, step ball or wire ball. We lived across the street from a school-yard lot which was especially good for stick ball or football. Tennis courts were two blocks away, and I played often enough to earn a letter in tennis in high school and college.

My father would take me to games in Philadelphia. He was a machinist for RCA in Camden and worked there for 27 years. In the 50's and 60's, after the Soviets launched Sputnik and the space race was on, they would make parts for U.S. government contracts. The parts would be assembled into rocket ships or anything else that would help with our defense during the Cold War. We would go to the Phillies, Eagles, and the occasional basketball game, back when the team was the Warriors and played in Convention Hall. It was fun. It wasn't frequent, though, because my father didn't have a car until 1962, so we would have to take a bus and subway everywhere, or go with neighbors.

I was a Phillies, Eagles—all Philly teams—fan. I believe that wherever you live, you should be a fan of that city's teams. Camden is across the Delaware River from Philly, so I did not like people who did not have an allegiance to Philadelphia teams. It was tough being a Phillies fan back then because they were always in eighth place. That is when the American and National Leagues were eight teams each, no divisions. It would seem that by July each year, the Phillies would be mathematically out of the pennant race. Still, when we went to games, I would yell a lot and keep score, keep track of what each player was doing during the game. My father would sit quietly; he could remember not only what a player had done in previous at bats, but exactly where the hits were. He had a great memory for statistics like that.

Somewhere in the late 50's, there was an NHL game on TV, and I was just mesmerized by it. It was before 1960, because in 1960 a team, the Jersey Larks, came to Cherry Hill to join the Eastern Hockey League. The Philadelphia Ramblers were playing in the EHL in Philly, but this team had come to Cherry Hill to play in the Ice House Arena, later called the Delaware Valley Garden. My father, knowing that I liked that hockey game on TV, got a job ushering the games along with a neighbor who had a car. I would buy a general admission ticket but would sit in the section that he ushered, which was right behind the goal the Larks attacked in the first and third periods. So I started watching hockey from that perspective. It also was good because I had the "behind-the-goal" anchor fence in front of me, as opposed to the people on the side who didn't have any protection. At that time there were only the sideboards and no glass or fence. From my perspective behind the goal I could see the joy on the players' faces when they scored and the offensive zone play was always coming towards me.

When I found out Philadelphia was getting an NHL team I thought it was great. I was in college and I didn't have the money or time to go to a game. I didn't follow them closely until I graduated college in 1970 and was teaching school. At the same time Bob Clarke came to the team. I began going to a few games, then found myself going more and more often. Like all good Philly fans I would yell at a ref or opposing player. Bob Kelly and then Dave Schultz and Don Saleski joined the team, and the games started to become more than games. They became events. I mean we were just beating people up and winning games. After being in eighth place for so many years with the Phillies and then their embarrassment of 1964, this was uplifting. We were not just winning a few games, we were really *winning*. We were beating teams so badly that some of the other guys didn't want to come back to Philly because they knew they would have to face our tough guys and our fans. It just grew and grew. It became important in Philly sports to have Flyers tickets and go to every game. In 1972 I was lucky enough to get season tickets in the second row, this time behind glass, in the end the Flyers attacked two of the three periods.

Back then, in the early 70's, if you went to a Phillies game in the middle of the season, it was just another game unless something unique was happening, like a career milestone or Steve Carlton pitching or Willie Mays or Hank Aaron were in town. Flyers' games, in that same time period, were different.

They were different because every time you went, as the Broad Street Bullies were building their identity, you had no idea what was going to happen. The personality and mood of the crowd was tuned to what was happening on the ice every minute, every second. We paid attention to everything and as a result, we were becoming more and more sophisticated about the game, and louder and louder. Everything the Flyers did was a milestone or unique, and every game was an event.

As I mentioned, in 1972 I applied for and got two season tickets. My dad would go to a number of games with me. It was great that I could take him to repay all the times he had taken me to the Phillies and Eagles. By then, the other NHL fans knew we were going to beat them one way or another, so we were increasingly hated around the league. At the same time we were loved more and more around Philadelphia. I remember Gene Hart once reporting when the Flyers were in Montreal that it was the largest crowd ever in the old Montreal Forum. He said that after having all those great skating teams and great goal scoring teams in Montreal, nothing had brought as many fans into the Forum as the Broad Street Bullies. This wasn't like baseball, football or Big 5 basketball; it was us against the NHL. The Eagles had not won a championship since 1960, the Sixers had not won since 1967, so when the Flyers won in 1974, beating the Big Bad Bruins—with Bobby Orr and Phil Esposito—it was special.

I was at both Stanley Cup parades. The first time, in 1974, I rode in a bus with the fan club and during the second parade, in 1975, I was with the Flyers organization. In both cases it was great to be in a bus since the people along the parade route were jubilant beyond common sense. The fan club ride was interesting because it started at the Spectrum and ended up at Independence Mall. The crowd just grew bigger and more intense the closer we got to the Mall. Many fans came out of work in their coats and ties. The fan club got together all of the old buttons they had and we would throw them out to people lined up along the parade route and there would be a mad scramble. The best part was watching three or four businessmen in coats and ties scrambling for an old Flyers' Fan Club button. This was another example to me of how important the team was to Philly and how happy everyone was to have a real winner again.

The players were accessible. They used to go to Rexy's after the home games. It was a bar on Black Horse Pike, just over the Walt Whitman Bridge in New Jersey. Bob Clarke had bought his first house not too far from there. These guys were from working class roots and were looking for nice houses, in nice neighborhoods, nothing fancy. So when he moved near Rexy's, it was natural to go to there. I guess the rest of the guys just followed him. After a game, there would be fifteen or sixteen guys there, minimum, eating with their wives. I got to know the guys from seeing them there and saying "Hi" or "Great game" before I started with signs. I think hockey players still have that working class background. They care about the fans and, although now not as accessible as in the past, they are still as friendly and as nice off the ice as ever.

On Mother's Day in 1975, Rexy's completely burned down as the Flyers were losing their third playoff game in a row to the NY Islanders. They had won the first three, then lost the next two and were losing Game Six of the series in Long Island. I was in Rexy's watching the game when the bartender said there was a small fire in the basement and everyone would have to go outside. So I grabbed my beer, my money and my date and left to move my car away from the building and onto the street. There was about 1:20 left in the game. We listened to the remainder of the game on the radio in the car, then got out and looked across the street to see smoke billowing out of the bar's windows and front door. I thought, "Well I guess we're not going back in there today." Everyone kept saying, "They always said if the Flyers ever lost three in a row this place would burn down." I still have the last mug that I was using that day. Rexy's was closed for a couple of years to rebuild and the crowd scattered to other places, but in the early 70's everyone went there.

I started with signs in 1972, about two months after getting my season tickets. If I yelled from my second row location, it would bounce off of the glass in front of me. My first sign was for Don Saleski, who looked like Big Bird from *Sesame Street*. At that time every team had someone nicknamed "Big Bird." Saleski was the best Big Bird look-alike of them all. Someone in the front row said that we needed to hold up signs for Saleski when the Flyers skated in front of

BRING
ON THE
MARTIANS

us before the second period. I got some markers and some paper and brought them to the next game and we held up signs that said "Big Bird." None of the other fans wanted to take their sign home, so I did. I brought them to the next game and in the first period, when he hit someone, I held it up.

After that I made a sign for Dave Schultz, and another for Bob Kelly, and one for Bernie Parent. Then I made one to mock the referee, then one to mock the other team's goalie and so on. People thought it was fun because we would score a few times and I would hold up a sign that read "Next Goalie."

As the Broad Street Bullies kept winning, the signs increased. In 1975, when the NHL announced that the Flyers were going to play the Soviet Army team, I made a large sign that said "Bring on the Russians." It was a total set up, knowing that we would continue to prevail and I would change the sign to read "Bring on the Martians." Fans mostly remember the one that read "Tell it to the Czar," which I used after the Soviets unexpectedly left the ice during a stoppage in the first period.

There have been so many signs. I have a few hundred at home and bring 90 to 100 to each game. I like the signs that are meant to ridicule the other team, like the "Start the Bus" sign. I use "Have a Nice Summer" when a team plays us at the end of the year and they are not going to make the playoffs. I especially like using that against the New York Rangers.

A sign that many fans remember from the 80's was "Illka Scorra Goalla" which I swear someone behind me had yelled after Sinisalo had scored a goal one night. Everyone also liked "Tocchet Rocket" for Rick Tocchet. Fans give me good suggestions and then I need to reduce their recommendations to three or four words max, to fit and be readable.

I think it is unique how the signs have led to many unbelievable experiences, like drinking from the Stanley Cup in the Flyers locker room—and filming it on Super 8mm film—after their 1974 Stanley Cup win. Another was when I was doing some work for *Hockey Night in Canada* in 1979. I traveled to New York for the Stanley Cup finals, and I made signs for the opening of the show. I arrived the night before and slept on a sofa in the suite that the *Hockey Night* producers used. The next morning everyone was in the room for a production meeting and I'm still asleep. I hear someone saying as he nudges me on the arm, "Sign Man, wake up, we have a meeting." I open my eyes and it's Bobby Orr. All I could think was "Wow, Bobby Orr is waking me up." He was doing the color commentary for the broadcast and it was five years to the day in 1974 when the Flyers had won the Cup, beating the Bruins and Orr.

One of my favorite signs is "Old Time Hockey." In the movie *Slap Shot*, "old time hockey" meant good skating and goal scoring. I started using the sign with that phrase after fights. So in Philly "Old Time Hockey" began to signify good skating, goal scoring— and good fights. And I think that's a key ingredient for Flyers fans. As long as we have guys that score, fight, work hard and are tough, they will be appreciated. I think that's all most fans want, a team that gives 100 percent every game. You don't see Flyers showing-off, like exercising in their front yard in front of TV cameras; they are fun-loving but not flamboyant. They play the game intensely and respect the fans. Philly people like that about the Flyers. Like my dad and other dads, they are still hard-working regular guys.

Ball

ANGELO CATALDI

"I'm positive the Red Sox killed my father."

My dad loved baseball. It was his biggest hobby. I can't even tell you why he loved it. I just know that by the time I came along, it was enmeshed in his lifestyle, and I became a part of that. He was a huge Yankees fan because they had Joe DiMaggio when he was growing up. It was the Italian credential. So I watched a lot of games. I can remember watching the 1957 World Series with him. I would have been six. He really listened to every game and got me involved. When I was a kid, he would leave me the score in the morning when I got up in real dark pencil. I can remember getting up and running over to the night table to see who won the game. This was when I was a real little kid. My mom, somehow the responsibility fell to her, would take me on the train all the way to New York, from Providence, which is about a three-hour ride, to go to games. She would always do it without complaint. So through the two of them, sports was in my blood, and I never lost it.

When my dad died, in the first paragraph of his obituary, it said "Angelo Cataldi, Sr., a lifelong fan of the New York Yankees." And I swear to God he died because the Red Sox won the World Series. My father was born a month before the Red Sox won a championship in 1918. They went 86 years before they won another one in October. He died in November. He was born a month before their first one and died a month after their second one. He hated the Red Sox. As he got older, he hated them more than he loved the Yankees. He would love when Pedro Martinez lost. And when the Red Sox came back from 3-0 in the playoffs and beat the Yankees, it was like a family member died. Now he was already ill, he had all sorts of problems with his kidneys, but I'm positive the Red Sox killed my father. After his death, when I wore the Yankee hat to the Phillies/Yankees game, I got murdered for it on air, but I was being totally sincere, it was a tribute to him. And when they won it last year, I was there for that, too. In the ninth inning, as I was standing there, I was thinking about my dad because that was the first time they had won it since he died. I knew that wherever he was, he was happy. That's the way it was.

Now my dad wasn't really excited when I became a sports writer. At twenty-two, I had gotten into serious journalism and was running a newspaper in the southern part of Rhode Island. Then I decided to go back to get a Master's degree at Columbia University. I had an advisor there named Norman Isaacs. He had just run the *Louisville Courier Journal*. I met him the first week and he said, "So what do you want to do?" At this point, it's all guys in the program who want to be foreign correspondents or run newspapers. I said, "I want to write sports." He really got pissed. He went, "What are you doing here? This is for serious journalism." And I said, "I love sports, and I love writing, and I'm thrilled I got in here. I'm good in school, so you're not going to get me out of here. I'm going to do sports." And it's fascinating because he said to me, "Alright, listen. Number one, you're not going to say this to anybody but me. They'll hate you here. Number two, if you're going to do sports, I don't want you to do it like anybody else did it. I want you to do it like a journalist does it. Can you give me that concession?" And I happily gave him that concession because that's what I was about anyway.

When I got a chance to work in Philadelphia, I said, "That's where I was born to work. They have the same attitude I do." I grew up in Providence, Rhode Island, where sports were huge. What made it big back then were the Boston Red Sox, the Bruins, the Celtics and, in my city of Providence, the Providence College basketball team. But I hated the sports culture in New England. It was really rooted in hero worship of the all-powerful sports athlete. I never looked at it that way. I always thought you covered a sport the way you covered City Hall. I hated the fawning that was done. I became persona non-grata up there because I took a philosophy of really negative, cynical reporting into sports that was not all that common. I got award after award, I mean I was very well decorated, and I moved up the ranks very quickly, but it didn't always sell well with the customers. It didn't always sell well with my bosses because they liked more of a hero worship kind of approach.

So I came here and from day one, I just loved it because if you play badly here, the fans boo the heck out of you. If you play well, they fall in love with you. But it was like you had to earn it here. You didn't have to earn it up in Boston when I was there. And I always felt like this was the best place for me to be and I've never felt anything else. You couldn't get me out of the city now. I used to say to my parents, "I should have grown up in Philadelphia." That's much more my mindset than small-town Rhode Island. About nine years later, I covered the Eagles during the first year of Buddy Ryan and I covered them the way you cover City Hall. I was bullheaded, tough, and I got into the finals for the Pulitzer Prize. And I felt that that day I had fulfilled my promise to Norman Isaacs, who had asked me to do it that way.

My dad was still alive when that happened. He was extremely proud because no one had ever been nominated for a Pulitzer for beat coverage of a sports team. That's the closest any sports journalist ever got for a Pulitzer award. Still my father's reaction to that was that while he knew that my being in Philadelphia was the right thing, he always wanted me to go back home. I had opportunities when I went into radio to get a job in Boston. I would say, "Dad, EEI is calling me again. They want me to come there." And he'd go, "Well, you should do that. You should do that. You should be closer to home. You should be back here in Rhode Island." And I would say to myself, "Yeah, over my dead body. I'll never do it. I'll never do it because I love it here." But beyond that, he never said much to me. My mom would say, "You know, he cuts out all your columns." And I went, "My father doesn't do that, my father would never do anything like that. He's a toolmaker from Olneyville." But he did. He had this amazing collection of all the stuff I had done. Never said anything to me. My mom used to say to me all the time, "Oh, he's always bragging about how you're writing columns and all this stuff." But he revealed very little of any of that to me.

I wanted to keep a journalistic perspective when I moved to radio. I thought I was going to, but I remember just before I left *The Inquirer,* I met with one of the top people at the paper. He said, "You know, there's no turning back; if you do this, your journalism career is over." And I went, "No it isn't." I said, "There's no reason why I can't take what I do here and apply it to radio." I was at the station about three or four days, when I got called in by the boss, Tom Bigby. He went, "Lesson one, kid. You're not doing journalism anymore, you better stop it on my station. You're going to come on the show, on your show, and you're going to inform, but primarily, you're going to entertain. This is a show business. You're in show business now. You're not doing that anymore." There was a period of time where I had to adjust. I had to catch myself a lot because I would start pontificating on sports. So there was a transition period, but I was working with Tom Brookshier, who was great at that transition because he was fun, but he was smart. He did both.

After a year or two, I just decided that, you know, that that part of my life was over, and that I had to do a whole different job in a whole different way. But I can lapse back. The one thing I maintain is the interview techniques I learned in journalism. That I still do. I do think it is probably my biggest strength. Of all of the goofy stuff we do, it's fun to go back to those techniques and to try to get the right question to bring out of somebody something that other interviewers didn't get. But it can't be a priority anymore. The priority is to make people laugh, to have fun with sports and to put it in its proper context— it's not life and death. It's just sports. That's the concept.

Still, I've learned that Philadelphia fans are very passionate. When you take a fan and you raise the level to ten, as high as it can go, that's Philadelphia for you. They want to be associated with a winner. A lot of them are working-class people who have difficult lives. They have bosses that are stomping on them and giving them a hard time and when their sports team succeeds, it's their moment in the sun, too. Their team becomes an extension of themselves. They can get a lot of positive reinforcement through the success of a sports team, like the Phillies right now. So many people are enjoying this 'cause they're so good. And people feel better about themselves when the Phillies succeed.

That has another edge to it, though. When they fail, there's an anger that gets more associated with the team because there's more of a personal attachment than you would get in a lot of cities. They are not all negative or all positive. They are both. So if your team is winning, they love you as no other city loves you. And you'll never buy a meal if you're a player on one of those teams; you'll be treated like royalty. But if you fail them, they will hate you, and you will get the other side, the backlash side of it. Now how you handle that will determine how negative they get on you. If you are kind of annoying about it, the way Donovan McNabb was, you're going to be on the upper level of the negative, and if you're a Mitch Williams type, who'll blow a whole season, but you handle it with such class and grace and humor, you'll be on the lower end of it. But if you expect passion in a city that loves sports, you got to understand that both ends are going to be higher. You're going to get more praise, and you're going to get more criticism. And that's all it is—it's all of it. It's not just the negativity. In Philadelphia, it's all of it.

And I love it here.

NICK BRADLEY

"I looked up...but didn't see him."

I started to play sports pretty young, at five or six. First, there was tee ball, then baseball. I did pretty well, hitting, catching, running the bases. My first real sport—the one that was *my* sport—was soccer. I loved to play sweeper and defense. In the younger league, I played goalie. I remember one time this big kid came down the soccer field at me and I dove down to get the ball. My dad had taught me to play as hard as you can and not worry about injuries. If you get hurt, well then you get hurt. You cut your arm, go get stitches. So whenever I play a sport, I play as hard as I can regardless of the situation. So when the big kid got close, I dove down to get the ball and got kicked in the face, but I held onto that ball.

It was my neighbor that told me about sled hockey. I was twelve or thirteen, but I was about to have surgery so soccer and hockey weren't my top priorities. I have arthrogryposis–it affects the lower muscles, bone mass and contractive joints. Some people can't bend their elbows and wrists. In my case, my legs only have 30% muscle mass. I can't bend my wrist and knee on my right side as far as my left side. Both my hips are dislocated. When I'm older I'll probably have arthritis in my hips. When I was two, I had surgery for club feet. Later, I had surgery on both my ankles. But it never stopped me from playing.

After the surgery on my ankles, my neighbor brought up sled hockey again. I started to play. Sled hockey is like regular hockey, but you play on a sled with skates; that way you can play on ice. Everyone is on a sled, so you don't see the disabilities, you don't realize that anyone is disabled. The sled has a front point to keep you balanced. You use two sticks to dig in and push the sled, using the same sticks to shoot the puck. In the beginning I wasn't real good. I had to adjust. After five or six months, I liked it a lot more because I became faster. I've been playing about six years.

NICK BRADLEY
#19
NICHOLAS
BRADLEY
USA
London Blizzard Sledge Hockey
ANNUAL TOURNAMENT

I wasn't as much of a hockey fan before I started playing because I didn't understand it as much, but now I think it is the best sport. It has the most physical contact. Every other sport nowadays you can't touch anyone without the referees calling a foul. In hockey you can hit players as hard as you can, knock them out and you keep on playing. I remember watching a video of greatest hockey moments, showing players like Dave "The Hammer" Shultz and Bobby Clarke. They were both tough players. They showed you had to be tough and have heart. I modeled my game after them.

My first practices were at a rink on Old York Road at six in the morning. My dad took me to all my practices and games, regardless of snow or whatever. He would take me even if the practice was at dawn and all he wanted to do was sleep after a week of painting houses or tending bar. On the way to practice, we would talk about hockey stuff. He would always talk about plays from the previous games. He was always there. I remember the one time I scored a goal and I looked up, but didn't see him. My dad was a smoker so sometimes he would be outside, but I would always look for him. So this time when I scored the goal, I didn't see him at first, but when I looked over again, I saw him there banging on the glass and I knew he was proud of me.

Then he died of cancer.

At first when he got sick with lung cancer, we would talk about sports. Then when he couldn't really understand anymore, I would just sit by him. At his funeral, there were thousands of people there. My dad was a painter and bartender all his life, starting when he was 21 or 22, painted our house inside and out. He was a real nice guy, looking to help others before himself, always lending an ear to whoever needed someone to listen to them. My dad was also a great coach. He didn't know all that much. He just liked to teach kids, and he knew enough for that. He knew it wasn't about winning or losing. Before a game he'd say, "Do your best and everyone have fun." I think he made an impression on them. He made an impression on a lot of people.

So when I joined the Jr. National team it was different. He wasn't there. And even though I knew my mom and brother would take me, it wasn't the best because scoring a goal in front of him is always the best, worth more than scoring in front of others. Now after I score, I think about him, look up and say thank you for the goal, but it's still not the best.

For the Jr. National team, I played goalie. We went all over—Canada, Rochester, and Chicago. Before my dad died, he would always give me pointers after games. He would always tell me what the other players did wrong, too. Now, it was different. He wasn't there. I kept my National team jersey. You get two of them, and when they collected them I told the guy I had lost one. So I figured I would give that one to my son one day.

I'm in college now, studying business and real estate. It's a two-year degree. I'm almost done. I still play hockey, not on the Jr. National team, but in a league. We just won the league championships. I am off that team now. After you turn 20 you have to move up to another team. It's in Aston, PA, I think. I'll play in this league as long as I can.

One day I do hope to coach my kids in basketball, hockey, soccer, and I'll drive anywhere to see them play sports.

ED RENDELL

"The shoeshine guy and the president of the bank both can have the same strong opinion about who the Eagles should start at quarterback. And the bank president's opinion is no more meaningful than the shoeshine guy's."

Growing up on the Upper West Side of New York, sports was a big part of my family. My father was the biggest sports fan in our family. He would take us to a ton of baseball games. We would go to Giants baseball games before they moved to San Francisco. He also took us to a ton of Giants football games. He had two season tickets so he would take my brother to one game and then me to the next game. I have great memories of going to those games with him. Unfortunately the game I remember the most is the game he wasn't there. My dad died when I was fourteen, a month before the most famous NFL game ever played, Giants vs Colts for the championship. My brother and I went to game, but it was very melancholy, knowing my dad wasn't there.

As a child, I played all the sports, but I wasn't any good at any of them. Basketball was my favorite sport to play because it was the most fun to practice. I went on to play both basketball and football in high school. I actually attended Riverdale High School, which was a big football powerhouse at the time. We were in the midst of a fifty-five game winning streak. Calvin Hill, who went on to become a great Dallas Cowboy football player, played there my senior year. He helped us to five years of undefeated seasons.

While I loved sports, my playing days were over when I graduated from Riverdale. Although I was interested in politics and government growing up, I never really knew I wanted to be in politics. I remember when I was in high school I could name all of the senators and that was a big deal. My dad, even though he was a businessman, liked politics and that only made my interest grow. So I always had a little bit of an affinity for politics, and I quickly found out that a political election is a lot like a sports game. It's a contest. There's a back and forth. There's an ebb and flow. In a sports game, the opponent does something and you react to it. It's the same thing in politics.

I still remember what it was like when I was first elected district attorney (it was the first time I was elected to anything at all for that matter). It was an awesome feeling. I would go on to be elected again after that, but the first time was very special. Hundreds of thousands of people saying, "You're the guy." That's a great feeling.

And while I enjoyed my time as D.A., my time as Mayor of Philadelphia was also a very fulfilling time. When I took over as mayor, the city was in deep, deep trouble. We were able to turn it around both financially and economically, and I think emotionally as well. That was a very fulfilling feeling.

My first real experience with the city was when I came here to attend the University of Pennsylvania. I didn't know anything about the city. During my time at Penn, though, I got to know the people. They're great people, hard working, and they're a lot of fun. I came to learn that Philadelphia sports fans, as anyone would tell you, are very rabid, but also very smart. They are fans who understand the game. They can be critical, but they can also be incredibly supportive. We can criticize, we can boo, but when there's effort, when we know the team is fighting hard, I think we're the best and most supportive fans in the world.

As Mayor I came to learn that a city with a great sports community is a city that has a heads up on others. First of all it helps the city economically, there no question about it. When the Phillies sell out a hundred straight games, it means there are forty-four thousand people in town buying things, eating dinner, doing all sorts of things. It's a huge help to the city's economy and it's a help to the tax base. When we're in the playoffs, it's two to three home games for the Eagles, it's seven or eight home games for the Flyers. It can be ten or eleven home games for the Phillies. Each game produces a significant level of tax dollars for the city. So it has wonderful economical benefits.

But the biggest thing about sports is the great emotional impact on the city. Sports unites a community. They can be a great leveler. We all have our opinion. The shoeshine guy and the president of the bank both can have the same strong opinion about who the Eagles should start at quarterback. And the bank president's opinion is no more meaningful than the shoeshine guy's. When the Eagles, Phillies, or Flyers are on a roll, it unites the community like almost nothing else can. It affects all people and it gives us a common bond. It can raise the spirits of a community like nothing else can. There's no question that sports can play a roll in unifying a city, especially Philadelphia.

My political career has allowed me to experience moments that feed my love for sports. It has also allowed me to do things I wouldn't have done otherwise. I now have a seat on the Comcast SportsNet Eagles Post Game Live show. They called me and asked if I wanted to be on it, and I couldn't resist. I remember doing the first show and I got thirty minutes in and I said, "People actually get paid for doing this! Sitting around and talking about football?" I was able to be at the game when the Eagles won the NFC Championship against Atlanta. I remember standing there with all the other fans knowing we were going to the Super Bowl. It was the end of such a long period of frustration.

But whether I am at the game, talking about it, or seeing its impact from the mayor or governor's chair, there is no question in my mind that sports is one of the most honest of human endeavors. It unites people for that reason. It doesn't matter who you know, it doesn't matter to who you are related and it doesn't matter how much money you have. What decides who wins or loses is what happens between the lines on the field, on the court or on the ice.

It's pure, it's honest and it's not affected by any cynicism.

It's a merit-based thing.

And I love it.

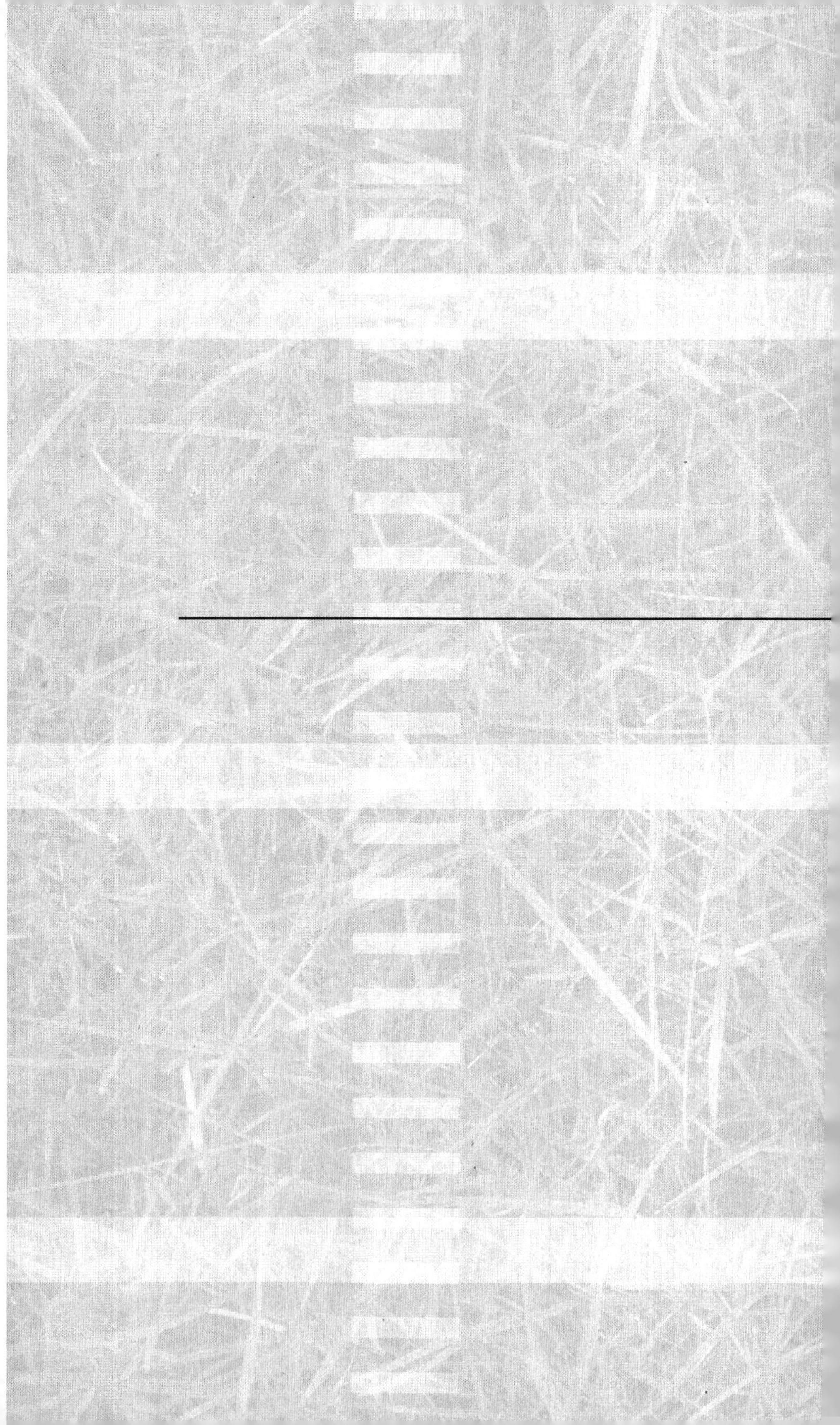

MIKE GOLIC

"So I said, 'Okay, if you are going to have these goals and this is what you want to do, I'm going to show you what it takes to get there. So are you willing to do this? Are you willing to sacrifice this? Are you willing to put yourself through what you have to get there?'"

I loved playing in Philadelphia. I played most of my career in Philadelphia. It was the best time of my career. One of the big reasons was it was before free agency, so all us were on the same team for a while. Now you get a little more movement. When I was here, there wasn't as much movement. So we had a big core of players that were together a long time. You really got to know each other a lot. And the fans were great, very, very passionate fans. Sometimes they may cross the line a little bit, but boy, did they mean well.

I grew up in Ohio, where you don't have the same passionate fans as you do in Philadelphia. But Ohio is, obviously, very well known for football. Lots of big recruits come out of there. In fact, if you grow up in Ohio and are a bigger recruit, the fans kind of ostracize you if you don't go to Ohio State. That's what happened to me. My brother Bob started it. He's six years older than me. He spurned Ohio State for Notre Dame. Then my brother Greg went to Notre Dame. Then I picked Notre Dame over Ohio State as well. So it was kind of a family thing. I enjoyed Notre Dame. I loved it.

When my first son, Mike, then my second son, Jake, went to Notre Dame as well, I felt unbelievable pride. I had told my sons, "You go where you feel comfortable," but they had goals set early on. So I said, "Okay, if you are going to have these goals and this is what you want to do, I'm going to show you what it takes to get there. So are you willing to do this? Are you willing to sacrifice this? Are you willing to put yourself through what you have to get there?" Just as my dad always told me, I tell my kids, "If you choose to get involved in something, I will be behind you a hundred percent and do all I can to help you achieve what you want." But that was the main thing, teaching them that it's going to take a lot of hard work, a lot of sacrifice. To their credit they did it. They stayed true to it.

I was very proud of them that they achieved that goal. I mean the first time I'm sitting in the stands, and I'm used to being out on the field, and here comes my son running out of the tunnel for Notre Dame, there's tears in my eyes. Then the next year, I got two sons running out of that tunnel and there are tears again, I mean it's just unreal pride and the pride is coming because it was their goal. They did all the work and made the sacrifices to achieve their goals.

Obviously, when your kid is playing, you really have something to root for, but I think football brings people together because it's a team sport. A team sport just naturally brings people together. It gives people a common goal to root for. A lot of people aren't going to go out and play in the pros. They are going to have to go out and get a job. I think in team sports, you get taught discipline, you get taught work ethic and you get taught teamwork. You learn how to rely on someone else and to work with other people. I think there is a lot of value in that, value that will carry you a lot farther than the sport you are playing.

ROB ENSLIN

"I looked up to athletes like the Broad Street Bullies because they knew how to handle danger. They responded by taking care of business."

I spent the first ten years of my life growing up in a suburb of Philadelphia known as Hatboro-Horsham, close to another small middle-class town named Ambler, in a nice home on Tennis Avenue. It was a neat street because, although it was less than a mile long, on one end you literally had the family that farmed all the corn fields that surrounded the area and, on the opposite end, you had people in the mansion, who would come out and dress their tree every year, and smack in the middle, there were lots of haunted places or barns where George Washington stayed on his march to Valley Forge. It was an idyllic place to be as a kid, lots of fields and trees and places to play. I had some friends, and throughout the year, we had this schedule where in the winter and fall it was football and street hockey, and in the spring and summer it was football and hockey with some baseball thrown in.

My mom was a stay at home mom. She was sick most of the time. I think by the time I came along, it just really threw her for a loop, so physically and emotionally I think she was dealing with a lot. My dad was kind of the strong silent type who kept the family together. But he traveled a lot. He was on the road maybe two weeks out of every month. He was a sales representative. He worked 35 years for a Canadian company, selling asbestos. At the time, asbestos was a popular material, so we lived rather comfortably. And then when things sadly fell apart in the mid 80's, when he was nearing retirement, he was laid off. He had put in 35 years with his company, but since it was a Canadian company, he was not in a position to file for age discrimination. The severance was a wash out. It was hard. But he was, and still is, a wonderful salesman. I am sure we talked about sports and, once in a while, we would play. But I think because he was older, and I was a wild kid, I think while his intentions were good, what he could do physically was very limited.

There was also the danger element, or at least the threat of danger, always running through my household. I think a lot of it was what my sister was going through, and my parents sort of fed off of it, and I, in turn, was thrown off by it. Around this time I was coming of age, but my sister was already well into her teenage years. She was the black sheep of the family, having a lot of fun at my parents' expense. A true flower child of the 70's, experimenting with sex, drugs, running away. We were on the police department speed dial. Even though it was painful for my parents and it fractured the family, deep down I saw something in my sister that was almost romantic. Wow, I thought, she's really living life in an exciting, bad way. I want to know more. Not that I would subscribe to such a lifestyle, but here she is off in her room listening to Led Zeppelin, Cheap Trick, Aerosmith and all these rock bands, and, I thought, if my sister's listening to them, they must be bad, evil and wrong.

So I think as a kid I had a caretaker role, my dad was away a lot, and when he wasn't, he was quiet and stoic. My mom was sick, gasping for air. My sister was getting picked up by the police. Somebody had to be in control here. So I was thrust into an adult role at a very young age, not knowing my up from my down.

So I latched on to Bobby Clarke.

Bobby Clarke was the patron saint of Philadelphia hockey. I believe he joined the Flyers in the early 70's, I want to say around 1972. He was a kid phenomenon in Canada. He quickly became their captain and lead them to two Stanley Cups, then became their general manager for a few years. I think whomever you ask, Bobby Clarke was the face of Philadelphia hockey. He always had the best interest of the team at heart, both as a player and as a manager.

I loved Bobby Clarke so much I asked people to start calling me Bobby. I figured Rob and Bobby, not much of a gap there. I wanted to curl my hair because he had a perm and it was in style at the time. And most importantly, he was missing his two front teeth. So I would ask my friends at school to knock them out. I mean I wanted to be him. I thought he was like a rock star. As a kid, my only other relationship to a celebrity was through the Beatles. My sports friends were also very much into music. Beatles first, followed by The Monkees, then Kiss. So I thought of Bobby Clarke as the John Lennon of the Beatles, and

Lennon as the Clarke of the Flyers. That was my whole world. If you weren't the Flyers or the Beatles, what was the point?

The Flyers were fantasy figures. People I wanted to be. I was smaller than most kids. I was smarter. I dressed differently. I ate differently. I knew right from the get-go that when I started school, I was different. I didn't really take pride in it. I almost apologized for it. I really latched on to these fantasy figures, these incredible figures who could do no wrong. I looked up to athletes like the Broad Street Bullies because they knew how to handle danger. They responded by taking care of business. Not that that was the way I would do things. I didn't have the courage to do it. I would have been scared to even pick a fight with somebody. But I saw it in pictures, I saw it in magazines, I saw it on TV, and I thought "Man, that's cool." I had a very romanticized notion of what these athletes represented. They were older. They were big. They were cool. They were just macho. And I think if there was a team at the time, not just in hockey but in all of sport, that represented this macho way of doing things, it was the Flyers.

They were the Broad Street Bullies. You had Dave Schultz, who was the NHL's penalty leader, who had a song "Baby … how long … will you keep me in the penalty box." It was a hit song on WFIL. I mean, the guy was a recording star when he wasn't out bashing people's heads in. They were tapping into that whole sort of dramatic theatricality of hockey, the physical gymnastics of it, and really, it was the Flyers. When you look back it was kind of ludicrous, but they sold tickets. It made for great theater and people kept coming.

Plus, my sister Deb and I had this mutual kinship for the Flyers. So when we were not off quite literally beating each other up, we would sit down to watch them. The Flyers were on Chanel 29, and I remember the grainy broadcasts because I would fiddle with the antenna. I remember them being on Friday and Saturday night around 8 p.m. It was usually just me and my sister watching. And she would "oohh" and "ahh" over the guys like Reggie Leach, and I'm there like wanting to be them.

My parents probably tolerated our interest in sports, at least us watching it, but I didn't think it was their bag. My dad, though, had an office in the house and I remember there was a business card sitting at my dad's desk, which was this mound of papers. The business card

was from one his friends who used to work for the Phillies. My dad said his friend was able to score tickets to Phillies games, and he asked if I would like to go downtown to see a game. It was like in Willy Wonka, finding the golden ticket.

When we went to the Phillies, it was a warm summer day. I don't remember who we were playing, I just remember that our seats were not very good. We were way up high. I remember looking down and being scared of having to climb the stairs because they were so high and so narrow. I think what I remember most, and I still get this when I walk in any arena, whether it is a major arena or a small one in Rochester, it's walking down into the tunnel, then the gates open and you see the field. You look down at these players, and calling them ants would have been a compliment they were so small. But it didn't matter; I was there.

I loved my dad dearly, and still do. I thought "Wow, it is pretty neat to be sharing this with him." And I'll never forget that. I think that's how my dad did, and still does, relate to me. It's not this overt emotional display that maybe we fathers now subscribe to. I think he showed affection by doing. And it was done quietly and in a very understated way. But if he talked to me the whole time, I couldn't tell you what he said, I don't remember any specific conversations. But it didn't matter. We were there. And I think it brought us together in a way that was a father/son experience that other kids have with their dad that I didn't get often, but boy was I getting it now. The whole experience of that game was crucial to me. And I like to think it was sports that allowed me to relate to my dad in one way, even if it was for this one short moment.

Now when I go to a game with my daughter, I think about what it's like to see it through her eyes. I hold my daughter tightly, almost like I don't want to lose her as a child. But I also in a way tap into the emotion she's feeling. Now maybe she's feeling nothing at all. She looks excited and cheers; she screams when they score. I want to experience that with her. I like to think my dad was thinking the same thing. It's not what as a parent I'm getting out of it, it's what they are getting out of it. If one of my daughters has a glimpse of what I had with my dad at the Phillies game, and she's talking about it 30 years later, then I succeeded.

BILL GILES

"At those moments, I would think of my dad. He would often say, 'Could you imagine the world without baseball?'"

I was raised in a baseball stadium.

My father was president of the Cincinnati Reds, so he needed to be at the park all the time. This meant if I wasn't in school or off playing sports somewhere, I was at the park. Growing up in the stadium, I got to know the ushers, the security people and the night watchmen, many of whom were African-American and Latino. I got to learn how these people lived and how to get along with anyone. At one point, I had the opportunity to go to a public school where you had to pass a test to attend. All the wealthy white children were sent there. Well, I passed the test, but my father would not let me go. He told me that when I went out into the real world, I would have to work with African-Americans, Latino-Americans. I would work with people who weren't wealthy, whose families don't have money. So he sent me to a big diverse high school. And I really think these experiences helped me later in life.

When I began to work in baseball, segregation still existed throughout the South. I remember when I arrived in Houston for my first major league job with the Astros; African-Americans could not go into certain restaurants and hotels. You would go to the ballgame and there would be a different restaurant for "coloreds," as they called them. Well, we had invited Willie Mays and Bob Gibson, two African-American baseball players, to come play. The Shamrock Hill Hotel wouldn't allow them to stay there. So we went to the city hotel and restaurant association. We said, "If you want to be a major league city, you need to not only let the black ball players stay here, but anyone who is black or not white come into your establishments." They were so used to thinking that blacks should not be mixing with whites, it took six months to overturn the policy. It was not easy to do. Once it happened, though, everyone accepted it.

Because of my dad, baseball was in my blood stream at a young age. Early on I wanted to be a ball player. As I got older, I would put on a uniform, go into the outfield and catch fly balls. At about 14, I finally woke up and realized that I wasn't very good, so I decided right then that I was going to become the general manager of a major league baseball team. From then on everything I did was with that goal in mind—that I was going to be the one who decided to trade a Jimmy Rollins or fire the manager. I wanted to be the final decision-maker. I began by working in the minor leagues in Tennessee, then majors in Houston, finally ending up in Philadelphia.

Of course, when I came to the Phillies, I still wanted to own a team, but I had no money to my name. Then in the late 1970's, I was having a drink with a lawyer. I said to him, "I'm kind of running the Phillies, but I'm not really running the entire team. With the current owner I won't ever really be able to call any kind of shots." He said, "You can buy a team." I said, "I only have like $50,000. How could I buy a multi-million dollar team?" He said with your expertise and good reputation, you can get a group of people together and lay out a plan where you will run it and own 10% of the team and operate it. Hopefully they will make some money off of that and enjoy the relationship with the ball players. Sure enough, in 1981 when the team came up for sale, I bought the team.

When I became owner and president, I was on cloud nine. It was something I had been wanting for thirty-some years. I know my dad would have been proud, and I thought about him as I built the team. He once told me that if I ever got into baseball that I don't want a pitcher who is under the finger of his wife, because if he is in the 8th or 9th inning, he will be thinking that if he doesn't get this guy out his wife is going to give him hell. She'll be thinking she won't be able to get that fur coat she wants. So he liked drinkers and hell raisers. That type of player fit well in Philadelphia.

Philadelphia is a blue-collar town. They don't seem to like pretty players, like Vaughn Hays, who was really good looking and a great player, but not very popular. They loved Pete Rose, John Kruk, anyone that looked like they were going to play first base for your neighborhood softball team. When I was putting the team together, I just said that this guy was fun to watch. Fun is a big word to me. I like to have fun. I like to see people smile. So I was attached mentally to players who are fun to watch. John Kruk is one of my favorites, the way he swung the bat, things like that. I like colorful players. And in '93, those players took us to the edge of a championship.

At those moments, I would think of my dad. He would often say, "Could you imagine the world without baseball?" He meant the ability to get excited over a Phillies game, reading about it, studying the standings, was an outlet for people. They don't have to worry about anything while watching a game. Being engulfed in the sports team you love is healthy for the mind. You also learn sportsmanship, teamwork, equality. Looking back, I think the world would be much more messed up without sports.

ome

ors

SHEIL KAPIDIA

"Sports has always been a way to bring people together. The consistency of it is important to people. When I was 6 years old, the game was always on for me to watch with my dad. When I was older, I may have been in trouble, but I still could sit down and catch the Phillies with my dad. It meant everything was okay."

Everyday after school, my friends and me would always play something.

It didn't matter what it was—football, basketball, baseball. You got off the school bus, go inside, change your clothes, come outside and play.

The little league games where I grew up in West Chester were very well attended. West Chester is a suburb about a half hour outside of Philadelphia. It's a nice area, nice high schools, nice school district. It was the kind of place where it was safe to play outside. All of the youth leagues in my town were at the YMCA. You saw all your friends on the weekends because everyone you knew was playing in the same leagues, whether it was hanging out waiting for their game to end or waiting after your game and watching them play. There was a lot of interest and a lot of parents there.

My parents never really got too involved in terms of coaching, though. My parents moved to America in the 1970's. My mom would watch sports with us, but she didn't really understand. My dad was a big sports fan, but he was never raised on the same sports—football, basketball, baseball. He didn't know all of the rules and fundamentals. My dad liked cricket, which is a huge sport in India. When I visited India, I saw firsthand what a big deal it was. It is on the same level of obsession we have with football here in Philadelphia. Seeing that showed me what a constant sports are in this world—it might be a different sport in a different place, but it doesn't matter, the obsession is still there.

In Philadelphia, people are raised on this obsession. When you're younger, it's such a big part of growing up. On Sunday, everyone knows the Eagles are playing or when the Phillies or Sixers are on.

It's a big deal. There is so much interest in the community. You can't go anywhere in the city, you can't turn on the TV or radio, or read the newspapers without the game being mentioned. You learn it from your brothers or sisters who were raised on it. They learn it from their parents. The cycle is never ending. If the Eagles win, Monday is bearable. If they lose? The whole next day is spent venting.

Sports has always been a way to bring people together. The consistency of it is important to people. When I was 6 years old, the game was always on for me to watch with my dad. When I was older, I may have been in trouble, but I still could sit down and catch the Phillies with my dad. It meant everything was okay. You go to college somewhere far away, but you come back to watch a big game with your family. You share these moments that don't change. Your relationship might be changing a little bit, you might be getting older, but the moments don't change. When I would first go to the games with my dad, he would drive. But recently we went to a game, and I'm driving home while he's taking a nap. I think it's the constant that's always there, no matter what is going on. You can always share sports.

Memories are built in those sports stadiums. My first experience of walking into the stadium is one I'll never forget. Walking into the Vet, through the concourse, I get that first glimpse of the entrance to the seats. I saw that green Astro Turf. Seeing all the players I saw on television, knowing I had all their baseball cards at home, and now they're right in front of me. It was an overwhelming experience.

I remember being with my dad at the "4th and 26th" game. It's Eagles versus Packers in the playoffs. I remember we were both sitting there and thinking, "Wow, they blew it again." We were both standing up. It was 4th and 26. I'm squeezing his shoulder, he's squeezing mine, because were both so mad. But then they completed the pass and we go crazy. I remember walking out of the stadium celebrating with him. It's moments like those only sports can create.

Now that I am a sports journalist, I truly see how far and wide sports touches people. One time I was doing an online chat during a game, and a reader named Tom was asking me questions about the game. He ended up telling me he was in Iraq, and this was the only way he had to keep in touch with the team. Sometimes in the industry, you think of what kind of impact you're having, but then you see something like that, and you realize how important sports are.

RAMI IBRAHIM

"My main thing is to make sure everything I say and do is right. This way they can see the image of a true Palestinian, a true Muslim, a true Arabian."

I am Palestinian, but I was born in Kuwait.

When I was four years old, I was kidnapped. My mom and dad went to a laundromat to get my father's shirts. They parked right in front of the store, steps away from the door. I wanted to go in with my dad, so I kept complaining until my mom said fine. She opened the door and let me out, then put the sun visor down and started putting on make-up. I'm knocking on the laundromat window, trying to get my dad's attention, playing around outside.

All of a sudden I see two Kuwaiti men, wearing long white outfits like dresses. I looked up at them and thought they were just playing with me, but they grabbed me and started running. I could see my mom, out of the car screaming for my dad, but I was gone, long gone. The next thing I remember it was late at night, the same day, and I was in a big rug factory, sitting in the back corner by myself, when I see these men, my dad one of them, come in and start beating up the guys who took me.

You see, my dad had connections. That was part of the reason, I was found the same day I was kidnapped. He was the Kuwait airport manager, working for the King and Prince. He also had a lot of connections with the police force. So he had a high position and was pretty wealthy. That's why we were respected and weren't treated bad. But Palestinians are not very well-liked in Kuwait. Even if you have a medical degree, you are brought in for manual labor. You'd be lucky if they'd even give you a job as a trashman. It's really bad. Over there, Palestinians are kidnapped as kids and sold. That is what happened to me. I don't know what they did with the kidnappers; I'd imagine they'd be put in prison, but then again they're Kuwaiti men so they are treated differently.

I moved to Philadelphia a few months before the first Gulf War. My three brothers were here, two of them studying at Temple University. We came over for a vacation, then the Gulf War started. My father was still there running the airport at Kuwait, but he left a week or two after the war started. I remember once he got here, he was watching television and he said to me, "Wow, this is not happening. It's as if it is being filmed in some factory in Hollywood." He had just been there, in the actual street in the actual area where things were being filmed. It seemed made-up.

But, in reality, we ended up losing everything.

We went from my father working with the Kuwaiti King and Prince to dealing with regular people. So at the beginning, it was hard. My father had nothing. He bounced around, tried a couple of things—a furniture store, a grocery store, corner store. Then we finally tried a pizza store that was successful, and we stayed with that for the next seven years. Luckily he was a strong guy because you see how it is now. When people lose their job, they go crazy. They end up killing themselves, killing their wives, whatever. And for him to go from having that much to having nothing and to still be strong in front of his family and children, that was big for me. I learned from that. I respect him for it.

We also went from having the best life possible for a Palestinian in Kuwait to living in a pretty rough area. I mean, in Kuwait, we were a respected family and the neighborhood we lived in was very family-oriented. Adults treat all children, whether the children are theirs or not, like they are their own. For example, if my mom and dad were outside and they saw someone else's kid, if he was doing bad, they would get on top of him, protect him, as if he were one of their own. That's the type of neighborhood and community I lived in as a child.

But, as I said, we ended up buying in North Philadelphia, in a neighborhood where the tensions between its Black, Hispanic, and Puerto Rican residents were high. One time I was driving with my mom and somebody spit at her for no reason. No reason. We were at a red light. My mom was sitting in the passenger seat and a woman just spat at her. And I was mistreated because I didn't know English. I didn't know how to communicate. All I knew was "yes" and "no." I was constantly picked on. So my family decided to put me in martial arts so I could learn self-defense and to keep me off the streets.

I started karate at the Golden Fist and soon started competing in tournaments. But I was constantly disqualified. In karate, when you compete, sparring against one another, the contact is like a light punch. That's it. That's the point, you can't hit. As soon as you touch, you have to back off. I didn't have that power, that strength, to have that self- control. My instructor decided that maybe it would be best if I went into a full contact sport. So they told me to try Muay Thai, mixed martial arts. Within a month, I had my first fight in a ring. I still remember before I came out into the ring, my trainer tried to get me hyped up. I remember him asking me "What is something that pisses you off?" And I'm like, "What are you asking me? What do you mean?" He's like, "Let's say someone stole something. What's something that you really care about that you would really protect and fight for?" So I said, "My bike"—my father had just bought me a bike. He said, "Okay, let's say that that guy you are about to fight in the ring, stole your bike." I got so mad that I came into the ring ready to fight. I actually lost the fight, but I came out happy. I lost my next two fights as well, then started winning. And ever since, I loved it.

It helped me in the neighborhood. During my first month at Golden Fist, I had six kids try to jump me at my elementary school. Six kids at once. I knew then that I needed martial arts to make it in the neighborhood. I took all six out with a technique where I had to punch and kick in the right areas, such as the groin, the throat, places where they would be out with one shot. The picking on me stopped after that. I think word got around. Those were pretty bad kids that were hurt. And it was outside the school, so everyone got to see it. After that, I didn't get in many fights in my life. I can count the times.

Then in high school, whenever my friends had a problem, they would turn to me to fight their fights for them. But my high school wrestling coach, Mr. Stevens, knew my friends were using me. One time he got word that I was going to be part of a fight going on after school. He grabbed me before class was over and took me to his office. "Listen," he said, "I know that you care about your friends, you got to protect them, you got to have their backs, you got to show your loyalty, but

WKA
CHAMPION
NEW YORK

your team is your friend to. Your team is more important because they have a good reason for you to be loyal, not bad negative reasons. You have to make a decision. You leave now and you are no longer part of this team. You stay and I will give you more respect. Now I'm giving you the option." Then all of the sudden, he looked at me and grabbed me. "You know what?" he said. "I'm not giving you the option. You're staying here. You're not going out. I'm not letting you do this to yourself." So I was like, "You know what, I'm going to take your word" and I stayed there. That was it. I never did anything for anyone on the street again.

I think sports teaches you that wisdom. It teaches you about love, about caring, about responsibilities, about family, because you feel like a family. One of my teammates, he struggled so much just to lose weight. He had to come in and lose ten pounds in a matter of two hours for the team. That's a sign of love. He really cared about the team. You know, sometimes my friends, they would lose a match and they would start crying. I would comfort them, give them a hug. Any other guy would think that was soft, not manly. Meanwhile I'm trying to show my bond to my teammate, that I care about him. That's love. We learned to love each other. Now whenever I talk to my coach or old teammates, before we hang up on the phone, we say "I love you, man" and "I love you, too." We really care about each other. We grew a strong bond we'll have for the rest of our lives whether we're seeing each other or not.

I was 18 years old when I turned professional. I was already fighting pro Muay Thai fights because there were pro rules, but I wasn't being paid. So I was like, I'm fighting pro anyway, I might as well legally do it and get paid for it. That was the main reason why I turned pro. In the beginning, I was fighting in Philadelphia, Delaware, New Jersey, Washington, mainly in hotels like the Holiday Inn and Marriot. In my early years, the crowds were small. Now I fight all over the world. I fight in stadiums with thousands of people.

But discrimination, racial tensions continue, just like in my old neighborhood in Philly. I used to have a Palestinian flag on my shorts when I fought, just to show my origin, to show that before I came into Muay Thai there was no Palestinian champion. Now I am that champion. That's big to me. That never happened until I came into it. But I took the flag off. There's an Arabian scarf, they sell it now in stores, white with black/blue. They got different colors now. They wear them as fashion in America. But my trainer, he doesn't let me wear it into the ring. I tried to come out with that Arabian scarf, but my trainer told me, "Don't' wear it. Don't let them know that you have this origin or that." So I don't wear it. It's hard. But racism exists.

As far as I'm concerned I'm an American because I'm a citizen. But that's not why I say it. Whether I have the citizenship or not, I've been living here all my life and I'm not going to live in a country and not respect it. This is my home. If I'm not going to respect it, then why in the heck am I living here? And I've been living here my whole life. I feel I'm an American because I've been living here as an American. If something happens in my area of Philadelphia I get mad just like everybody else. So I consider myself an American, but, with all that said, my nationality, originally? I'm a Palestinian.

But I'm at the point now, in fighting, I hide my Palestinian identity because they treat me so bad. I'll give you an example. They always cheat me in my fights. They rob me. You would never see anybody as professionally respectful as I am in the ring. I'll show you videos where I drop guys and then help them up. That's how far I would show respect, but the judges are so against me. I don't know what I have to do to get them to like me. I think 9/11 is a big part of it. I was coming out for a fight in New York City right after 9/11. I was fighting for the United States Championship, but everybody kept chanting "USA, USA" or "Go back to Iraq." I'm not even from Iraq, I don't even know anyone from Iraq, but everybody kept saying "Go back to Iraq." That's the kind of thing I went through. I've been fighting for America, representing them as their champion. I beat that guy up so bad, but in the end they made it a draw.

Still, everything that I have accomplished is due to by brother Mohammed. If it hadn't been for him introducing me to martial arts, I never would have become who I am, not just as a fighter but as a human being. It was my brother Mohammed's idea. He's the one who brought it up, enrolled me in it. He's the one who's been following me and taking me to my fights. If I have a fight in Florida, he'll fly with me. If I have a fight in New York, Niagara Falls, he goes. He's the main reason I'm doing what I'm doing.

Mohammed taught me one thing. He made me believe in what I wanted and encouraged me to go after it. I remember him teaching me math and I would do a problem and whether I got it right or wrong, he'd make me feel like I got it wrong because he wanted me to think about and believe in my answer. Like I would get a right answer and he'd say "No, it's wrong." And he'd get in my head, making me think it's wrong. And he'd say, "See, you don't believe in yourself. You didn't know the right answer. If you did, you would have said that that was the right answer." And he tells me the truth. He doesn't sugar coat anything. When I fight, whether I win or lose, he tells me like it is. And I respect that. I learned a lot from his truth. He made me strong. I have a lot to thank him for. The way I think now for my age is pretty good compared to other people my age. My mind is pretty disciplined and I have him to thank for that.

Now I bring these experiences in to my gym, Sitan Gym. I have a saying here: "Sitan Gym, where you learn more than punches and kicks." I talk to my students like adults, whether they are three years old or fifty years old. I talk to them about life, about discipline, about respect. I'm always giving them examples from my life and the lives of others. My main thing is to make sure everything I say and do is right. This way they can see the image of a true Palestinian, a true Muslim, a true Arabian. Because I'm sure that what they see in the movies and on television is different. I'm dressed in a shirt, jeans, fashionable clothes. Meanwhile when most people think of an Arabian, they think of a person dressed in a long dress sitting on a camel. They think we disrespect our women. I'm trying to show them something different.

I give women the most respect when they come here. Whether they are young or old, I treat them the best. I talk to them in the sweetest way. Guys, they think we're ignorant. I talk to them kindly, I show them that they are worth something. They've never been treated the way I treat them. This is my way of telling them, by showing them. I don't tell them I'm this or that, I show them. My actions speak for me. Some people like it, some people don't. They're like, "I'm coming here to work out." But I think I've changed my pupils' lives. The way they think. The way they talk. The way they act. I also try to make Muay Thai not just an individual thing. You fight now, but you stay for everybody else. It's like a family. You go to any event, they'll tell you, the gym that shows that family model is Sitan Gym. We always come together. We support each other. Win or lose, we support each other. This is what I'm about. I'm more than just a champion. I'm more than just a trainer. I do all I can to change people's lives for the better, and to me, that is true success. God gave to me, so I want to give back. I grew up with the knowledge that I should measure success by how many people I blessed.

That's my way of giving back.

BOBBY CLARKE

"The only thing I ever valued is that 'hard work will beat talent every time.' If talent won every single time then what would be the point of working. You can always beat talent by hard work."

Flin Flon was way up north, a small community of ten to twelve thousand. For someone like myself who loves sports, it was the perfect community. We played hockey all winter; and even though the season was short, baseball and swimming in the summer. We had no television until I was twelve or thirteen years old, so every kid played every sport. Families were bigger in those days, so there was always a ton of kids to play sports and that was really all I wanted to do—play sports.

It was mostly pick up games, kids showing up on the outdoor ice playing hockey. Whoever showed up, played. We did have Saturday morning hockey games that were organized by the community, with everyone on a different team. We also had our all-star teams, who would go down south about 500 miles and play Winnipeg. So, of course, for those games, it was us against them—small town from way up in the north playing those spoiled guys from down south, not that we really knew them. We'd just want to beat them. The year I played, we had a lot of really good players. We would go down there and wax them. It was a great feeling to come down from Flin Flon and beat those "spoiled brats."

The community I grew up in was working people. Everybody worked. So I knew nothing different. My dad was very uncomplicated, very quiet, but he always said, "You get nothing for nothing. A man has to work." There were no ifs, ands, or buts in his mind about that, "a man has to work." So my dad had me delivering papers when I was eight years old and working at the service station while I was going to school. I was never without a job. I never thought of it as work, either. It was what I did.

My dad was a miner. He grew up as a farmer, my grandfather was a farmer, my uncles are farmers, but when my dad turned 18, he went to

Flin Flon because he could get a job there working in the copper and zinc mines. They'd go down underground with their diamond drills and drill holes in the rock, pack 'em full of dynamite, then blow it up. Then somebody else would move it out. He was pretty adamant about me going to college. He used to say, "I have to work with my back, but you don't have to work with yours. You get a good education." But as it turned out, I quit high school in 10th grade and went to play for the Flin Flon Bombers.

The Flin Flon Bombers were the team every kid wanted to play for growing up. The NHL was too far out of our vision to think we would play for those teams. Because we didn't have TV, we had no vision of the NHL, just Saturday night hockey on the radio. So we knew Gordie Howe, Maurice Richard, and those guys, idolized them, but we wanted to play for the Bombers.

The Bombers players worked in the mine in the mornings, practiced in the afternoon, and the company paid for eight hours. It was a pretty good deal. It was the mine paying for entertainment for the employees. The reason we couldn't go to school when playing for Flin Flon was we'd go on two-week road trips. Our closest rival was Brandon, about 400 miles away, then Winnipeg, which was another hundred. Edmonton was probably six or seven hundred miles. Then there was Calgary. So when we went out, we went out for a long time. There was no time for school.

My dad was not a happy man when I told him I was quitting school to play hockey. He said, "You better make sure you are making the right decision." But after that, there was nothing he could do about it anyway since I was 17 years old. I had lots of friends who quit school and went to work in the mine. Good job. Got your check every two weeks. That was good. It wasn't like at that time I was going anywhere in hockey. He didn't know I was going to make the NHL. I was a really good junior player. Like I was probably, I don't want to sound like I'm bragging, but I was probably the best junior in Canada for my age. So I assumed that other coaches had told my dad I probably could make the NHL, but we never really talked about it much. I didn't even know if I'd really make the NHL. All I knew was I was going to play junior hockey and see where it took me.

I didn't know if having diabetes would hurt my chances of making the NHL. I think I was thirteen or fourteen when I found out I had diabetes. I don't know what life is like not having it. I didn't want to talk about it when I first turned professional. I wasn't ashamed, but as far as I was concerned it didn't affect my life. I was playing hockey and that's all I wanted to do. I wanted to be a hockey player with diabetes. Yet anytime anyone wanted to talk about it, it was always the diabetic hockey player. For me, there was a huge difference. Being a diabetic hockey player gives you a built in excuse to play crappy, but I'm a hockey player and I have diabetes. If I play crappy it's because I play crappy, it's not because I have diabetes. After my first five or six years playing, when I'd proven I could play and was good enough to be in the NHL, I didn't mind talking about it.

Later Mr. Snider, owner of the Flyers, told me that they were in the second round of the draft and Jerry Melnyk, a real close friend of mine and chief scout for the team, kept telling them, "You've got to draft Clarke. You've got to draft Clarke." The other teams had passed me by because they said, "He's diabetic. He can't stand the rigors of the NHL." But obviously the rigors of the NHL weren't nearly what they were with Flin Flon. You weren't taking the bus to Los Angeles to play. You were flying out here. This was luxury. So Mr. Snider called a doctor who was a diabetes expert. He said as long as he takes care of himself and eats properly, he'd be fine. So the Flyers drafted me.

In 1969, the Flyers were a really good defensive team. They had great young goalkeeping with Bernie Parent and Doug Favell. They had some really good hard-working players. Their problem was they didn't score too many goals. That was two years after expansion, though, so it took them a while to get enough goal-scoring players. The first three years in the league were tough for me. We missed the playoffs, were out in four games, then missed the playoffs. The following year, they had hired Shero, which may be the best decision this organization has ever made. Then the Flyers traded for Reggie Leach and Rick MacLeish, as well as drafted Bill Barber. All of a sudden you have all these really young players to go with Ed Van Impe, Joe Watson and Gary Dornhoefer, veterans who were still twenty-eight, twenty-nine years old. So they were players for us. It was a great mixture. It just took Shero a couple of years to get us to do it right.

Also, when we brought in Dave Schultz, Andre DuPont and Bob Kelly, we started physically abusing the other teams who had been physically abusing us for a couple of years. The way I came through sports hockey was that you had to be tough, and if you were tougher, you had a chance to win. When I played junior hockey, the Bombers were really tough. When I first came here, we weren't tough. We used to get abused. Other teams would bang us around. But all of a sudden, we were tough again and we were knocking them around. We also had enough talent. You can't just beat somebody up, you have to also score goals. But if you are getting beaten up physically, you are not going to win in hockey.

Philadelphia was a tough workingman's city. And that's the type of hockey we were playing and people loved it. Whether we were following the city or they were following us I'm not sure, but it seemed to be a perfect match. It was like we all had a little inferiority complex and were kicking the other guys' rear ends. I never heard our players use the expression *Broad Street Bullies*, but I think it probably was a title we tried to live up to. Sometimes we went overboard doing it. It was part of the whole image that we had. And it was helpful.

I had a fair number of friends on opposing teams, but it would never change the way I played on the ice. I would never expect them to change the way they played against me. It was hard. My only exception would be, I felt really strongly and still do, that as the superstars, those who had been in the league for a long time, got older, they had earned the right to have your respect. I played against Gordie Howe when he was older, and that was as close to god as I will ever get. And I thought, I better respect that man.

I was really lucky with Gordie Howe because I played with his son Mark, who used to live two houses from me. So Gordie and Colleen Howe, the grandparents, would come see their grandkids all the time. I had a daughter going to school with one of Mark's kids. My daughter, four or five years old, would come home and I remember asking her, "What'd you do today?" and she'd say, "We were riding on Grandpa Howe's back. We were playing horsey with Grandpa Howe." My idol was on his hands and knees playing with his grandkids. How wonderful is that, eh?

Now Philadelphia is home. When I first moved here, I lived in an apartment in Barrington. There were a lot of Navy people and hockey players all living in these little apartments. For my first couple of years I'd just go to the games and come home. Or I'd stop and have something to eat at a diner, maybe go to Rexy's, which was owned by a buddy of mine. There wasn't much of a social life the first couple of years. It was hard. It was hard. This is a big city for someone coming out of a city of 10,000. I mean, Flin Flon had single-lane highways. You come down here and the bridges have more cars on it than the whole town of Flin Flon. It took me a while to get comfortable.

Later I became part of the community. And even after I was well known, I could still take my kids to the ballgame, play ball, talk to the parents, and just kind of be a part of the neighborhood. It was so good, not only for me, but for our whole team. All the young guys had kids. Kids were in school, in Little League, into a variety of stuff. Most of us at that time couldn't afford to have two houses like the athlete of today. We lived in this community. We were part of the community. I think it was really good. At least in my time, it was really good. Obviously I'm a lot older now, but I feel comfortable in this area. This is home.

The only thing I want to end by saying is I've never liked athletes who write a book about themselves. That's pretty egotistical, I guess. Who cares? You were an athlete. You had a great career. Congratulations. Good-bye. I think that's how sports are supposed to be. It's wonderful to be remembered, but once you're done playing you got a life to get on to, not think you are so important as to write a book about yourself. I hope that this is not going to sound that way. I hope I'm not bragging or talking too much about myself.

3

GARRY COBB

"A lot of kids do not value an education. I explain to them that they can play ball, but if they get hurt, what happens? An education is something they are always going to have."

Growing up, I followed my older brother James everywhere. We grew up in a big sports community right outside of New York, where we both played little league baseball. I never played with him, though. I played against him—all the time. And he hated it because his friends would say, "Little Cobb is going to be better then you, he's four years younger and he's already hitting the ball as far." It would burn him up. But I was learning from him. I was learning from his buddies. It was making me a better player.

When I was younger, I could really throw a baseball. I pitched a lot. I would throw no hitters, perfect games. I probably pitched too much. I would end up pitching 12 innings a week because I would pitch one game and then in the next game, the kid would get in trouble, and the coach would have me pitch.

As successful as I was at sports, my dad wanted us to get an even better education. My dad dropped out of school when he was in 8th grade. School wasn't the big thing back then; the big thing was working on the farm. My grandfather encouraged him to drop out. So my father worked and worked. He didn't go back to get a high school diploma until he got out of the army. While in the army he learned the value of an education because the only guys who were promoted had a high school diploma. His experience of going back to school to get his diploma was one that really affected our lives. It taught him the value of education and he wanted to make sure we understood it as well. He vowed that all his children would go to college. That was no easy task, however, because there were seven of us—three girls and four boys, including myself.

I attended Stamford High School. While there, I went through some challenges school wise. As a black kid, you weren't supposed to be doing well from an educational standpoint. They would call me "Uncle Tom" when I did too well. But my pop kept demanding that I get an education. He reminded me to not get in trouble, to do my work. He always made sure I was preparing for college.

During my time at Stamford, I played basketball, football and baseball. There was hardly any time of the year when I didn't have practice. I believe that one sport helped me in the other sport. The agility in basketball helped me in football. The aggressiveness in football helped me in basketball. Baseball helped with my hand-eye coordination in all the sports. The fact that I knew I had to get a scholarship in order to go to college pushed me harder.

After a while I knew I was going to play in college. I started being recruited when I was a sophomore. My brother got an athletic and academic scholarship to Dartmouth. So I wanted that as well. When it came time for me to choose colleges, my dad wanted me to go to Princeton. But I knew I wanted to play professional football after college, so I chose University of Southern California (USC).

I was infatuated with USC. They were on TV. They won the national championships. They had great players. I knew I wanted to go there. During my time at USC, we won one national championship and two Rose Bowls. The experience of running out of the tunnel during those games was completely exhilarating.

But I knew getting an education was important. During my first year at USC, I got distracted by the beautiful weather and the girls. The football players were very popular on campus. We didn't have to join fraternities—being on the football team was enough. The longer I was in college, though, I learned how to do things on my own, such as staying on schedule. These were things I learned after I got serious about my academics. Ultimately, I graduated with a degree in sociology.

And as fun as the football memories are to me, those are not my best memories of my time at USC. During my time there, I developed some great relationships with the players and other people I still keep in touch with today. I met my wife there. In fact, my happiest time at USC was knowing my dad was on cloud nine during his trip to the Rose Ball and that he was floating on air during my graduation. My mom and dad sacrificed so much for us. I was happy to make them proud.

I got serious about school. I also got very serious about football. I realized I could play in the pros. I was playing against guys every day who went to the NFL. I said to myself, "I am beating these guys in practice all the time." I knew I could play on that next level as well.

I remember the day I was drafted. It was day two of the draft. I went much later then I thought I would go, because I was injured my last year. It was a discouraging experience. I was wondering if I was going to get drafted at all. Then I got the call telling me I had been drafted by the Dallas Cowboys in the 9th round. The Cowboys were coming off of a year where they lost to the Pittsburgh Steelers in the Super Bowl. Everybody knew the Cowboys. During that time, they were on TV every week. They were called America's team, and they really were America's team.

During my first training camp, I'm standing there, and I couldn't believe it. I am here standing next to Roger Staubach, Tony Dorsett and Drew Pearson. These guys were household names and now I was on their team.

But I got cut at the end of training camp.

I had never been cut before. It was a crushing experience because I thought I had made the team. I had made it to the final cut. That was something that really hit me in the gut. It gave me more drive than ever before. I was going to do everything I could to make sure that didn't happen again. I signed on with the Detroit Lions and played both special teams and linebacker. I was trying to knock somebody out every practice. I knew I had to make an impression immediately. It didn't matter if it was practice, I was trying to knock out every guy I could to make the team.

Then after six seasons in Detroit, I was traded to the Philadelphia Eagles. They needed a linebacker, and they traded Wilbert Montgomery to get me. People were not crazy about the trade at first. After a while, though, I started to get a good response from the fans. People in Philadelphia are very serious about their football, and so was I.

During my time in Philadelphia, our children grew up and connected to the area. We planted our roots here, and we weren't going to leave.

I try to instill the same values in my children which my Mom and Dad put in me—the value of hard work, the value of education. My son went to Stanford to play college football. The thing I liked about Stanford was that they believe in education first, football second. They also had a good football team, and they went to the Rose Bowl a couple of times. It was a lot of fun. I got the chance to see him play in quite a few games.

My experiences growing up, remembering all of the people who have helped me, have also made me want to get more involved with helping inner city youth. My dad was always there for me, but for a lot of kids, their dad is not there. Without my dad, I don't know what would have happened to me. He was my disciplinarian. We had fun together, but he also challenged me to be a better player. Getting to the point where I could eventually beat him in sports was a lot of fun.

I want to share that with kids. So I am involved with a number of programs which help youngsters. You get to see a youngster gradually get his or her life together. Some of the guys I've worked with are now adults. I remember when they were kids. Now you talk to them as young men and you see that they have developed and grown. That's exciting to me. I like seeing it in my kids, and, of course, in the kids that I work with. So I like trying to motivate people, talking to people. I enjoy the chance to share something with people that might help them, motivate them, to be the best they can be in their lives.

A lot of kids don't value an education. I explain to them that they can play ball, but if they get hurt, then what? An education is something they are always going to have. That message is what I tried to convey when I wrote my first book, *Don't Be Clueless*.

I wanted to teach people like my father taught me. Make sure ~~to~~ you set your goals, have a purpose in life, try to treat people the way that you want them treat you and live a good life. Learn what it takes to be successful in life. Learn that you have to set a plan of what you are going to do. You've got to be willing to work. You've got to be diligent about your life.

I like to tell kids, “If you are going to do something, be serious about it. Don’t just go through the motions. Do your homework because you never stop doing your homework. Regardless of whatever it is you do, you got to go home and learn your craft.” I know as an athlete, especially on defense, you study the offense. You study what they like to do in certain situations. And sure as day, a lot of times during a game, you are going “Oh boy, this is the situation I prepared for. They are in the same formation they use to run a certain play and the guy’s moving, and the quarterback’s getting ready to throw the ball, then when that happens, ‘boom,’ I’m going to step in there and get an interception.” That’s the way you have to be. You have to be diligent about your business. And if you develop diligence, it is going to give you a chance to be successful.

I think that is one of the reasons I love sports. It’s a competition where the best person gets the prize. It’s got nothing to do with favoritism or your background. It’s all about who can get the job done. The person who works the hardest and wins gets all the glory that comes with victory.

I think people love that.

HERMAN DOUGLAS

"I was like 'I ain't quitting. Forget that. I don't care how hard. I'm not quitting. You know, cause I'm no punk.'"

I was the first generation to ever experience video game systems. When the sports games came out, you got a different sense of the players. It transitioned from baseball and football cards to actually seeing the player's ability and vicariously living through the video game. You could act like you're that person. So we became video game freaks. We played every sports game out there. At that time there was no online playing, so everybody came to your house to play video games. You would actually have a tournament with five to ten people in your bedroom playing on a black and white television, trying to beat each other.

But we still played sports. We fell in love with the game before video games came out. We actually watched television—the type with rabbit ears and vice-grips on the television to tune the stations—to learn about the game. We had beta video recorders. People would actually record the games and look at what athletes were doing. We watched Dr. J shoot hoops or Michael Jordan slamming on somebody. We saw Randall Cunningham, being one of the first black running quarterbacks, dropping back and just crushing people. We wanted to master those skills. We figured out that we could do that by practice. So we would go out and try to emulate their moves.

Kobe Bryant and LeBron James, that's all they did. They copied. If you were to cut off their heads and just watch the motion of how they play, it would be like Jordan. You know, it's okay to copy, as long as you're copying the right cat. That's a skill. Find someone who is doing well in a sport that you would like to do as well in. Watch his videos, read his books and copy. We did the same thing.

We knew with work we could be good. That's why we did it. But we knew there was no shortcut. You can't shortcut the shortcut. If you want to be better at shooting some hoops, you had to go out there and actually shoot hoops for hours. Hours. If you wanted to be good at wrestling, you had to take them down at practice. I remember blowing out my knee, then as I recovered, just doing suicides back and forth to get my wind up so I could be better, stronger, faster. It was in you. Sports shows you how to be a champion, how to be better at things, how to gain a work ethic. Sports shows you how to work towards a goal. That's what it has meant to me. It gives you the opportunity to use a lot of the techniques and philosophy from sports to instill into your children or other people's children.

Like my coach, Ernie Haggert. He's still alive today. Just thinking about him brings tears to my eyes because he actually saved us. He actually taught us. I remember in track there was someone who was running the 400, but he hit the wall at 300. At 300 yards, your body is exerting everything, and you have to use arms and legs to pump through. Most people can run at least 200 to 250 yards at full steam, but the last 100 yards are the hardest yards ever. People feel like they are doing to die. So here we are, and Haggert says, "Listen, a quitter always quits, and a winner always wins. Which one are you?" You know, he used to say things to us that would stick in your mind. "Are you going to be a winner or are you going to be a whiner?" Just little clichés that would make you listen. He'd say, "People quit football, you quit piano lessons, you quit school, you quit everything. You know? You a quitter? I don't want quitters around." He would say things like that to us. I was like, "I ain't quitting. Forget that. I don't care how hard. I'm not quitting. You know, cause I'm no punk."

During that time, the 80's and 90's, crack was hitting the street. I had a crack house right next door to my house. We used to see all the guys, the local drug dealers, line up their cars after school down at the courts. They would have Jettas, Hondas, Saabs, with these rims and a whole bunch of money. They would wear these chains, these whole big ropes. We used to look at them like "Wow." They used to play basketball and they were real good at that. But now they were also selling drugs to, like, your mom. We actually had friends who had drugs sold to their moms. Coach Haggert would say, "They don't have a future. They're just selling drugs. You know they're quitting on themselves. They don't want to, but they're just quitting on themselves."

Then he would have someone like Kevin Scott come to our practice, also in a white Saab. Scott would talk to us, saying, "Listen, I sell drugs." And we would be like "You sell drugs?" And he said, "Yes, I sell pharmaceutical drugs. I'm legal. I went to college. And they didn't go to college. Yes, they probably make more than me now, but you can't look at the short term; you've got to look at the long-term. I have real estate." We were like "Real estate? What's real estate?" He'd say, "I own my own houses. I work for a pharmaceutical company. See these drugs right now? I actually get paid a hundred thousand dollars a year for pharmaceutical drug sales." We were like "What are you talking about? For real?" And he said, "Just think about it. What do the drug dealers have to give their kids? What do they have to help their family out compared to me?" And then you looked at how the dealers were living compared to him. It actually helped me and a lot of my friends. Out of my crew, a majority of us went to college or into the military because we had these engines to show us the way. They showed us a different world.

Now I'm older and I can't play sports anymore. My knee is banged up. My back is jacked up. I can't do anything without hurting the next day and paying for it. I get to lift weights, but that's not the same as going out there and getting to play ball with your son. Every time I play with my son, I feel it for a week. You know your mind is saying that you can go faster, but your body is saying it can't go. Your body is not moving any faster. My kids chase me, and I can't shake them sometimes. It was hard for me. I was running around one day, and I couldn't shake my son. I used to be able to shake anybody back in the day. My mind and my body weren't working together. It's gone.

Today my favorite moments are watching my kids playing sports. It's that moment when they do something good in sports and they smile and go "Did you see that? Did you see that?"—just to see them basking in the glory of winning. Sometimes, the only thing you really want growing up is the recognition that your parents say "good job." Not seeing your dad at something like that, it just deflates you. Your dad is your hero growing up. So not to see your dad, it psychologically messes with your mind. And it's like "wow, I'm not good enough, I'm not worthy enough for my father to come see me." I'm probably real extreme with regards to having a championship mentality, but for me I wonder, if I'm not there with my son making sure he's going to be good or do what he has to do, then who's going to be there?

And now as a teacher, I see the impact ever day that not having a father has on somebody's life. I have had little girls cry in front of me and say things like "I don't know why dad doesn't love me." "How come my dad is not here?" Or some people say, "Dad says 'I wish you weren't born.'" Just things that hurt your heart, that are so destructive to a person's mind. If a father were there, the problems we have in our society would cease to exist.

Parents, teachers, coaches, we're all role models, and the kids are copying us.

ALYSON GOODNER

"We wanted to be the best. We didn't want to be the best inner-city team. We didn't want to be the best most-diverse-team. We just wanted to be the best."

My first meet was at the Philadelphia Cricket Club. I was three and swimming in a six-and-under race. I would have to just get one lap down the pool. I wasn't supposed to swim, but I said I wanted to try. So my dad stood on one side, my mom on the other, and they basically pushed me in the pool. I loved it. By the time I was nine, I was outgrowing the Country Club League so my dad started entering me in United States swimming meets. But I was swimming unattached, which meant I wasn't part of any team. Somewhere along the way, I met a young girl by the name of Bridgitte White and we became good friends very quickly. Bridgitte swam for Jim Ellis and the PDR swim team.

At the same time, my father, who was a real observer, would come to these meets not only to see me, but also to watch the teams. He wasn't necessarily observing which team was the fastest to dominating the others. He was observing coaches and how they interacted with their swimmers.

You see, my dad was a public school boy. He went to public school his whole life, but my mom and my dad made the choice to send me to one of the premier local private schools, The William Penn Charter School. Therefore, when he was scouting a team for his kids, while he was looking for a coach that handled swimmers well and a team that had a family feel to it, he was also looking for a team that had gender, class and racial diversity. He was looking for a team like PDR. So my dad spoke to Jim Ellis and said, "I really want to give this a shot." Soon after, my mom and dad said, "Listen, we are going to take you over to PDR and have you jump in the water and try it out, see if you like it."

My first day of practice, mom drove me down to Nicetown, Germantown. My mom was this 5'1, 95-pound woman who drove a massive Suburban; she was the epitome of the little woman-big car syndrome. We trucked down to Nicetown and parked outside the Marcus Foster pool. Bars on the window, graffiti-covered, we knew we were no longer in Chestnut Hill. My mom turned to me and said, "Okay let's get in there." I looked at her and said, "You don't need to walk me in." I was this totally spunky ten-year-old. I told her "I'm good, I got this. Don't worry, Bridgitte's inside, I'll be great."

I could tell that my mother was scared. She had initially gone along with this idea because my dad really wanted it. However, she was the parent who was born and raised around Philly and knew the neighborhoods really well. I knew she was concerned, but I said, "Let me go in. I'm going do this on my own." So she let me go in alone.

I definitely went into Marcus Foster thinking, "Well I'm a good swimmer and everything is going to be great. We're going to get along wonderfully." In the past, when I would join a team at Penn Charter or when I would join a team in Chestnut Hill, it was all "rah rah!" Everywhere else I had swum or gone to school, people had known the Goodners. My father was this larger than life personality and my mother was the most generous and caring person in the halls, on the field or on the deck. My brother was a shooting star, I mean he was just a star in everything that he did. The minute I walked through that door, though, it wasn't this warm and fuzzy welcoming. I wasn't going to be able to rest on the laurels of my family. I knew from the minute I walked on deck I would have to prove myself here.

When I joined PDR, I was one of the first people from a white upper class neighborhood who started looking at the team. There was already a group of great black female swimmers, such as Valerie and Vanessa Patterson, Akida Stevens, Kelly Arnold and Alicia Times. Those were the matriarchs of the pool and rightfully so. They were getting the job done in a really powerful way. These girls were about business. They were probably thinking, "Here comes this new girl. Is she even going to stick around? Is she really going be able to hang here?"

So it wasn't warm and fuzzy. It was more like, "If you're here to perform and work hard, and make the team better, we'll give you the time of day, but you need to first show that you're not gonna just up and leave." It was definitely a new experience for me. I realized quickly that this is where I would get to make my own identity outside of my family. It wasn't just "You're a good swimmer, so we're gonna love you." That wasn't good enough. I had to give respect to get respect It was really this reciprocity of respect and relationship that made PDR the family that it was.

The turning point for me, knowing I had become a solidified member of the PDR swim team, was the Black History Meet in DC the summer I was 11 I was maybe one of only two or three white people at the meet. I had won the high point trophy for my age group. I was worried about it. I went to Jim and said, "I don't know if this is necessarily appropriate that I'm winning this award at the Black History Meet." Jim responded, "You're part of our team. It's absolutely appropriate. You swim for PDR, you represent our team, our culture. This is who you are, it is who we are."

That night, after the swimming was done, there was a dance. I love to dance, always have. I was out there dancing with all my teammates, having a good time. Some kid from another team got on the microphone and said, "Stop the music, there's a white girl on the floor." I don't know why he said it, maybe just to taunt me. I was a pretty easy target. I was the only white girl on the floor, and I was not necessarily subtle. The DJ pulled the plug and stopped the music. When that happened, my whole team rallied around me. It was amazing. I remember all the boys—Jason Webb, Attiba Wade, Damon Small, plus Valeria, Vanessa and Akida— all went up to the front of the room to find the source. They said, "Listen, this is our team. Back off." Everyone knew who PDR was, respected the team and listened. That was the moment when I understood what Jim was trying to get me to understand earlier that day. I was watching all of my team back me up and embrace our differences, our diversity, our identity of PDR Swimming.

I think when my dad was choosing role models for me to be around, he thought, "She's got some wonderful teachers and people who really care about her, but I want her to be around somebody who finds opportunity when maybe it isn't obvious, because she's been in a lot of places where opportunities are obvious." He wanted me to be around somebody who can really take a situation and make more of it than people think is possible. He wanted me to see that adversity can be a profound positive because it makes you stronger, it allows you to figure out plan B, it allows you to push yourself to go further than what you thought was possible, it makes you redefine your limits or remove them altogether.

Think about what Jim and PDR was accomplishing. They were winning meets, going to Nationals, endlessly producing athletes who were ranking top in the nation, all with a pool that was six lanes in a deteriorating building with cracked windows and walls. But Jim didn't give you any time for excuses. There was never any doubt in his mind that we were there to do something great.

I mean, three-quarters of the time when we were there in the winter, we had no heat. We had a couple of hot hoses running into the pool. But if you complained, he said, "Get out of the pool." I mean that was it. You're done. There were just no excuses. It was that quality that drew my father in, made him see, "Look, here's this man who's been given probably the most sub-par facility in the city and look what he's doing with it." And for me, that removed any possibility for me to be like "Oh, I don't have x, y, and z so I can't get it done." I absolutely know that if my family had never made that decision to put me in that pool and expose me to an environment where you take what you have in front of you, work with it, and make it better than what anyone thought was expected, I'd be in a very different place right now, in my career, my relationships, my life.

The legacy of the PDR team is that there was this little space where kids from every socioeconomic level and every race walked through the door at Marcus Foster and didn't lose that identity, but used it to make a great team. I think that's a real interesting distinction. In Hollywood movies about integrated teams, they talk about being "color blind"—nobody sees color, but that's not it. Jim actually highlighted our differences because that's what made us a stronger team. The fact that I was coming from Penn Charter with a family that had x, y, and z opportunities and that another swimmer was coming from only a ten-minute drive away and had different opportunities (or the lack thereof), those differences were highlighted, respected, seen and heard every day. Jim wanted us to hold on to that—those individual pieces of ourselves—but also to recognize that we were part of something greater than ourselves, and that those things about us had to not yield to the team, but instead communicate with the team. Together we created one big and brilliant story.

So we all walked into Marcus Foster with our differences and our collective diversity in all of its best color, texture and qualities, and when we got in that pool, we created our collective identity, the PDR identity. This identity was stronger than any other team out there because it was so diverse.

And as a team, we had a super simple goal: We wanted to be the best. We didn't want to be the best inner-city team. We didn't want to be the best most-diverse team. We just wanted to be the best. The fact that we were super diverse was one of the essential elements that was going to get us there. Jim created an environment where we naturally bonded with people that we were so different from, and that doesn't happen, you know? Jim's acknowledgement that regardless of what our backgrounds were, regardless of where we were coming from, we all had our own skills, our own strengths, we all had our own issues. He never said one was more significant or severe than the other. He acknowledged the fact that in the future we were all going to have different types of issues and some were going be harder than others, and that what he could give us more than anything was this attitude of "no excuses," that you can rely on your teammates, and that when adversity comes, the best you can do is look it in the eye and say, "Okay, bring it."

CHRIS PRONGER

"I think the camaraderie of the team is what got us through that year."

I grew up in a pulp and paper town.

What's a pulp and paper town? I'm from a town of 6,500 people. The local mill employed the bulk of the town. Summer time is fishing. Winter time is hockey. Very cold, a lot of snow—your typical small Canadian town.

For me growing up, it was really all about hockey. My friends and I, yeah, we went to school. You do your schoolwork, attend classes, you do all that stuff. But for us, hockey was number one. We'd wake up in the morning and think about hockey. Then after school, we played roller hockey, played on the outdoor ice rink. We practiced all the time.

I think that sport is pretty much ingrained in Canadians' minds. You know it's very rare that you find a kid who hasn't played or at least tried hockey.

I loved playing in hockey leagues growing up, especially because I lived in a small town. When you're from a small town you play with a lot of the same kids year in and year out. You know, I think because we were such a small town, we didn't play each other a lot. We played the surrounding towns a lot. You kind of have to, because when you're playing on the outdoor ice rink after school, that's kind of where you learn your skills and you learn all the fun things. And then you learn the structure of hockey during the games.

Growing up playing hockey took a real group effort from my family. It's a lot of work. There was a two-year age difference between my brother and me, so we never played together on any teams. My father,

Jim, and mother, Eila, did everything they could for us. You got one parent going one way, the other parent going the other way, and you know, it's tough. It takes a huge commitment from your parents to allow you to play a sport, and I was fortunate enough that they put in the time and effort to take me to practice, come watch me play, all the rest of that stuff. And at the same time, both worked. So it took a huge commitment.

My dad taught me how to play, and I picked up some things from him, but I really learned a lot about the game on Saturday night.

Every Saturday night was hockey night in Canada. I was able to pick up an awful lot just watching the game on TV. But I put a lot of time into learning about the game, too. I read a lot of books about different drills and understanding what the drill is trying to accomplish. I used those things to make me a better player.

My hard work began to pay off when I was 15. I signed with the Stratford Cullitons. I wasn't paid, but it was my first time signing with a Junior B team. In Canada, the competition to sign different players was so intense that you had to sign contracts at a young age. Otherwise teams would sign fifty guys just so other teams couldn't sign them.

Signing with Stratford was a big commitment for my family and me. It was a twenty-hour drive from home. It was a long ways away, and you leave at 15. It was tough. Not all players are ready for it, and it was obviously a big step up in competition. I was 15 years old, away from home for the first time, playing against twenty year olds. It was different.

Thinking back to my days coming up in the hockey system in Canada, I laugh at the things that go on now regarding hazing. Nowadays, the stuff that goes on is child's play compared to what used to happen to us back then. I got my nuts shaved, I got my head shaved. Forced to drink and do all that stuff. It was certainly intense. But my time in Stratford made me a better player.

After my first year, I went and tried out in Peterborough for the Peterborough Petes, a team in the Ontario Hockey League (OHL). My brother had gone the U.S. college scholarship route, and that was kind of the route I was leaning towards. But Peterborough flew me down there to kind of check out the community, the city and their program. I wasn't sure if I was going to fit in with the style of play, but I really just kind of fell in love with the place. I fit in. I didn't feel out of place, and it was just kind of a natural progression for me.

After two years with the Petes, I was drafted 2nd overall in the NHL draft by the Hartford Whalers. I had all my friends and family with me at the draft in Quebec City. The build-up to the draft was pretty fun. There were a lot of trade rumors and jockeying, but Hartford moved up from the sixth pick to the second pick to select me. It was a lot to go through as an 18 year old, especially looking at all the different possibilities for trades, which teams are looking to move up to get you and all the rest of that stuff. So that was pretty interesting, and a pretty fun start to my career.

Draft night was fun, but being the second overall pick, I felt the pressure almost immediately. Obviously they'd moved up to pick me, and I was coming into a team that was struggling and needed to improve. They needed to make the playoffs and show some development. It was a tough situation to go into. It's kind of funny looking at it now, but yeah, there was definitely a lot of pressure and you know, a contract that I signed and expectations and all the rest of that, it was tough.

My first two years in Hartford, I made some mistakes I'm not proud of. Being only 19, and playing with some players into their 30's, I wanted to fit in. I remembered my days in Stratford, the hazing, the team bonding. So I went to bars with my teammates. But I also got in fights. I got arrested for a DUI. The pressures of being in the NHL got to me at a young age, but I did have some success while in Hartford. To this day, I still remember my first goal on Ron Hextall.

After my second year, I started to bounce around a little bit. I was traded to St Louis, then to Edmonton. I finally ended up in Anaheim for the 2007 season, where I won my first Stanley Cup. It was a euphoric moment that was 14 years in the making, 14 years of blood, sweat and tears in the NHL. The culmination of a long season, the journey that we took to put ourselves in that position and ultimately win was very satisfying. All of my family and friends were at that final game. All of my buddies were in the locker room afterwards, sipping out of the Stanley Cup. You know it's funny, you talk to different teams about what happens after they win, and it's a closed room where it's just the players, or it's a closed room where it's just family and friends. But ours was just a free-for-all. Everybody was there. I mean we had like 500 people in our room; it was a quite a show.

You also hear all types of different stories about what people do with the Stanley Cup. You get dogs eating out of it and guys sleeping with it. I didn't feed my dogs out of it, but my kids had cereal out of it. It kind of becomes a nice little party favor. You're able to throw pretty good parties when the Stanley Cup is going to be there.

After three seasons in Anaheim, I was traded to the Philadelphia Flyers. I knew almost nothing about the city before I came here. I played out in the West for fifteen years, so I didn't know a whole lot about Philly. But playing in the NHL, you hear about the fans and the passion that they have for the game, their sports and their teams.

It didn't take me long to realize that what I heard about the city was true. One thing that makes Philly such a great sports town is the sports complex. You have the Wells-Fargo Center, the Linc and Citizens Bank Park all right next to each other. Everybody congregates in the one area. It's pretty unique; not too many cities have that.

Making it to the Stanley Cup finals my first year here was quite the experience and an introduction to the fans. It was kind of a rare season where you have so many ups and downs. At one point we were in 14th place, and we got a win in a shootout to get into the playoffs in the last game of the year. Then the next thing you know we're down 3-0 to Boston, and we come back to win that series. Then we're down 2-0 against Chicago in the finals, but we come back and win the next two. After all we went through, to lose two heart-breakers to end the finals the way we did, it was tough. It was a lot of fun, it was great being involved in it and giving ourselves a chance to win, but very disappointing that we weren't able to finish it.

I think the camaraderie of the team is what got us through that year. That is what sports gives you. Whether you play baseball, hockey, football, any of these team sports, it takes the mentality of everybody pitching in for that one goal. At the end of the day it boils down to winning. It's not always the main focus, but it seems to always come back to this—you have more fun when you win. And when kids come together, they can see that. They see that when they play as a team and play as a group, they win. Kids start to get it. I think they understand, alright, I need this guy to do this job, I need to do my job so this guy can do his job. You know, it's fun to see when the light bulb goes off and they kind of start getting it, and how much fun they can have just enjoying the sport because then they just start playing the game. They understand it's a team game, team concept, and they just play it hard, play it fun and the rest takes care of itself.

It's been a long ride for me in the NHL. I once was that kid learning how to put it all together, doing drills and reading to make myself better. To think I've come from those long bus rides in Canada to where I am today is a testament to my hard work and my family. From being the 18-year-old draft pick to now having two kids of my own, to being in the locker room after we won the Stanley Cup to now having my kids visit me after the games is great.

One motto that has always pushed me was to "play every game like it's your last." As cliché as it sounds, it's true. You never know when your career's going to be cut short or when your career's going to be over. You have to enjoy it, really enjoy it. Enjoy every moment you have because at some point it's all going to be over and you're just going to be another guy who used to play the game.

5

LEONARD WEAVER

"What God does for me is to remind me that when things aren't going well to continue to have a smile on your face. Continue to press on. That's what God teaches us—to continue to press on."

I grew up in Florida, which was basically your typical hood-ghetto-slum project. A lot of violence, a lot of drugs being sold, a lot of gang-related activity. That was pretty much the environment I grew up in. But we also had our little backyard games. We did kickball, baseball. We played a game where you throw the ball in the air, one guy catches it, and you have to run touchdown to touchdown without being tackled by anyone. It was pretty cool, kind of formed a lot of good skills from playing those games.

My first organized sport was football. Later, in high school, I also played basketball and ran track. In basketball, I was a shooting guard. I was the kind of guy who pulled the trigger and scored the points. That was my job. In football, I played linebacker initially, then quarterback. I actually played a little bit of everything, but those were my initial positions. A lot of it was predicated on what we needed that week. I was one of those players the coach felt that he could put in different positions, according to who we were playing and their personnel.

I was heavily recruited out of high school. At first, you get the handwritten letters and the phone calls. Then you go on campus visits. I was recruited by Steve Spurrier at the University of Florida. So I went to some games at Florida, went to their campus, did things like that. They never offered me a scholarship, though. They wanted me to walk on, but I decided not to. I also went to visit Oklahoma State, did a couple of things there. Then after a while everything kind of stopped and I was kind of wondering what I was going to do. I ended up going to Carson Newman College, a Baptist college. I wasn't a party guy. So I just sort of stuck to my grades, stuck to hanging around with just two or three guys. Together, we did a lot of gospel music concerts.

I also did a lot of bible studies.

What God did for me then, and does for me today, is to remind me that when things aren't going well to continue to have a smile on your face. Continue to press on. That's what God teaches us—to continue to press on. There is a verse that continues to keep me grounded to this day, Corinthians 4:13. As a matter of fact, I got it tattooed on my wrist. It says, "I can do all things through Christ who strengthens me." Understanding that it's never me. He's given me the ability, but it's God that's given me the power and the steadiness to accomplish the goals and the things that he does. Continue to press on. I understand that, man.

For instance, in college I made the transition from linebacker to tight end. It was tough. I never played tight end before. They wanted me to beef up, gain thirty pounds, and still be explosive and run, which was kind of difficult. But I was able to make the transition. I was able to use my speed to catch the ball and run and beat defenders. I earned All American honors. I give God the glory for that.

It's when I received All American honors that I first thought I could play professionally. I was getting calls about going to the All Star game and being a prospect for the NFL. At that point I kind of felt like, all right, this was my home. But I figured I wasn't going to get drafted, so for me, I knew it was going to be a little bit of a different route.

My thing was to think of it as just an opportunity, an open door. My mental attitude was to just work hard, just bust my tail. I got up in the morning when no one else was getting up. Worked out, went to class, worked out again. Just prepared myself for the opportunity. And then, when I wasn't drafted and became an undrafted free agent, it didn't make me feel any less. It actually made me feel like I was entitled to work even harder because those guys who got the money first, you know, they came in, they got the stuff, kind of made me feel like "Man you got to continue to work." And that attitude has never stopped. It's actually been the sole foundation of my success. When I was younger, my parents weren't together. And my mom was a big influence. The thing she did which kind of forced me to grow up more as a young man was *work*. She had to work to make sure we had. So I would have to say that her work ethic and her heart to survive, to keep us living, was probably the biggest thing that drove me— she showed me how to continue to press on.

When you're an undrafted free agent, you get an opportunity to look at where you want to go. I choose the Seattle Seahawks because they didn't have any one else competing for the fullback position. It was Max Strong and nobody else. I had gotten feedback at the All Star game and at the Cactus Bowl in Texas from a lot of NFL scouts that I was too small to play tight end and I wasn't quite fast enough to be a running back. So they said, "Why don't you just try fullback?" So I said, "Why not? Hey, there's an opportunity. Just go ahead and take it." And from there, I just did it. I saw that there wasn't much competition, so I took it.

Still, training camp and playing professionally was a shocker, a shocker and a wild moment. because not only are you around guys you saw on TV, that you see win championships, and that you see commercials of, but it was just the overall experience of the game. It's faster. It was very physical. It was definitely a big difference. I remember my first NFL game, coming out into the Superdome in New Orleans. That was an unreal experience, man. It took me back to the *Jerry McGuire* moment where it's like "Wow, this is actually happening." I also scored my first NFL touchdown. It was quite an experience. I never actually thought that I would get an opportunity. Mike Holmgren called the play "36F." I actually remember going through a couple of guys, breaking a couple of tackles, and when I crossed the touchdown line, I was in awe. It was an unbelievable experience. It was sweet.

My second year, I had a high ankle sprain and actually missed whole season. To me, man, it was painful. It was very frustrating because as a free agent you don't get many opportunities. I was definitely scared because I had a family and I didn't have any stability. So I was worried. But you know, man, I just began to pray and God just kind of gave me a sense of calmness and security that no matter what happens "I gotcha." From that point, I just began to give back to the community. I started coaching over at the local high school, giving some of the skills and talents that I learned to those kids and that community. Turned out to be great for me.

Now that I'm in Philadelphia, I've started Weaver's Workers in Camden, NJ, where I teach reading, writing and character essentials to kids from 8-15. A lot of the kids are underprivileged young black men or so-called "ghetto kids." These are the years when kids are deciding what they want to do with themselves. It's either they are going to be taught by someone who can influence them or they are going to be taught by the streets. So I think that it's very important for me to teach our young black men that there is more to life than sex, drugs and rapping. I think it's important to teach them that you can be a good individual with character, to understand that there is more to life than those things. You can actually be somebody. I want to let them know that no matter what the hood tells you, you can become more. That's my giving back not only to our young black men, but people across the world. That's what I preach and teach when I talk to people. I wanted to give back to our young men, letting them know that no matter what the hood tells you, you can become more.

One thing I've learned from this work is that kids know when an individual is being real. Nowadays, we have a lot of people who come in to talk to kids, but they've never experienced that kid's life. A person who grew up in the suburbs has no idea what it's like to grow up in the hood. So when you are talking to the kids, they can tell: "Dude, you can't tell my anything because you grew up with everything. So you can't tell me about a struggle." Somebody who has been in the struggle, such as myself, who is now successful can tell them, "Dude, I've been around the drugs. I've sold the drugs. I've run the streets. I've been in the gangs." Those are the things I can tell them and they can experience that, like "Dang, this is a guy who has done everything I'm doing and he changed." So that let's them know change is possible. That's what it's all about.

That's why I think that I relate to these fans. I understand the blue-collar attitude of not getting anything, but working for everything. You appreciate things when you work for them, when you understand why you're working for them. That's the attitude I have. That's why, I think, we relate as fans. They understand Leonard Weaver is a doggone hard worker. That's the bottom line. If he isn't successful at anything, he's going to be successful at hard work.

I think that's a common experience of football, the struggle, the fight. You're talking about a 4th and 1 situation. So many people out there deal with a 4th and 1 situation in their life, whether it's paying that last bill on time or whether it's in their marriage, fighting each other. It's that struggle I think everybody gravitates to, that they can see. The player who is running the ball has to get that one yard. He's struggling.

So I think that people gravitate to that moment, and they're interested. "I know what you are feeling even though I'm not on the field. I know what you are feeling." People gravitate to that commonality. So that's why I really think people love the game. That's why we relate. That's why I love the fans here.

When I made my first Pro-Bowl, after joining the Eagles, I cried, man. Andy Reid gave me a call. I was on the way to the movies with my three sons. I pulled over and actually just started crying. And my sons started crying because they've seen me, they've come to my workouts, they saw how hard I work. It was, man, a blessing. It was a true blessing. I thanked God all the way from the movie theatre until I got to the press conference.

I've held my oldest son back from playing football. It can be a life-long beating. I'm kind of trying to preserve his mind. But I'm going to put him on a team this fall. He wants to play football. His total choice. I've told him, "You want to do it, you can do it." So I'm going to let him play. I'm looking forward to it. And I'll be there at every game that I can be at as long as my schedule permits.

But before he thinks about making the NFL his goal, I want to let him experience the game, kind of let him be the judge. My son is very smart. I've been teaching him about understanding humility, what it is all about. Just play the game with pure heart and love. Those are the simple things I tell him. It's almost unreal to me every time I hear I'm the highest paid fullback in the NFL. Sometimes I almost want to block it out because I don't want my mentality to ever change. Continue to be who you are because it has gotten you this far. So continue to be that person. Love and humility. That's kind of what I've been living on.

JAMES ELLIS

"And if we are going to be PDR swimming, then we are going to represent the city."

When I started the team, there were gangs and kids were afraid to go in different neighborhoods. They were talking about how they shouldn't go to North or South Philly. They were talking about how you don't cross over into certain neighborhoods because that's the Barbary Coast gang's turf. So I wanted to do something positive. For me, starting a swim team was my way of giving back—of remembering the support of family, teachers and community members who allowed me to cross over so many bridges.

When I started coaching, I found out there were other teams in Philadelphia. So I looked at the recreational teams. They were okay, but I wanted our team to be more than "okay," I wanted us to be *excellent*. My team was going to be the best of the best. I wanted to compete on the highest level possible. I wanted my kids to be able to make it to the Nationals. I wanted my swimmers to go to the Olympics. I saw that there were no other teams trying for that goal. People think about PDR and say "Oh that is the first black team." We weren't the first black team by any stretch of the imagination. We may have been the first black team that put in our mission statement that we strived for excellence. Our program was designed to take kids to the highest level. That set us apart from everybody else.

My belief was that since we had this gorgeous pool at Sayre Recreation Center in West Philadelphia, if a kid wanted to make the Olympics, he shouldn't have to go across town to Germantown Academy, an all-white team, to achieve that end. That had been the m.o. for most grade school swimmers who were African American. Somebody discovered them and then a white team gave them a scholarship to join their team. They were removed from the black community and swam on the white team where they eventually assimilated to that lifestyle. They were no longer role models in the black community. So, I wanted to do the reverse. I wanted my team to be so good that the kids would stay and become role models in their own community, let their community enjoy watching them perform their task.

In the beginning, it was important to think about the team as an African-American project. It was introducing the sport of competitive swimming at the highest level to the inner city. And the fact we were an African-American team helped the white teams and parents go through an evolutionary change. In the beginning, they were like "Don't let those black kids beat you." Then as they saw we weren't going away, people starting embracing us. They started saying, "They don't come with their pants down around their butts, earrings in their ear, and with a boom box." They started thinking maybe these are some different kids than we are seeing on the news.

See, in the beginning, we encountered outright racism. For instance, we went to a swim meet in Delaware. We sat our clothes and bags and things up on the deck, then we went in the water to warm up. When we came back to where we had left our things nicely folded, our stuff had been piled on the floor near a drain. That was a derogatory move. And making it worse, there was a group of women sitting right by. I knew they did it, because we didn't do it. And we were not going to take it. That's why it was mandatory for parents to participate in my program, so that when we traveled, there was a group. Parents could protect the interest of their children. They could see what was going on. They could get involved. People really did things that weren't going to be in the best interest of their children. I wanted them to see it up close and personal.

At other times, I had to lead by example. My kids and my parents were going into a different environment. I knew that all eyes were on me, so as a coach I had to "walk the walk and talk the talk." I had to go in unafraid, assured and confident. My swimmers needed confidence to swim that way. My parents needed to feel that way sitting in the stands. They were only there because of me. So it was my job to put down that psychological image for them, a positive image, an image of confidence. I remember going to a swim meet at Newtown Academy. There was another team there called the Tiger Sharks, and they were sitting in the corner. I walked in and looked at the lay of the land and

I said, "I'm not sitting in the corner." They always want black people to go to the back of the bus, the back of the restaurant; well, I am not going to the back of the bus, the back of the restaurant. We are going to sit right here, so to speak, at the 50 yard line, at the middle of the pool. We are going to sit on this side because the stands are on this side. We want everybody to sit there and look at us. That is where we are sitting. I see you sitting anywhere else, you are getting dressed and you are going home. That is where we are going to sit. That is where we sat.

In the beginning, we got a couple of medals and ribbons. We weren't winning big time. We got a ribbon for maybe 15th place. Over the next ten years, though, we improved. We began to be known for getting kids off to college, getting kids to reach Junior National time standards. We started breaking some records. I had a young man who set a record in 1988, in the ten year old and under category, for the fastest 50 meter breaststroke. That record stood for 19 years. Even now, he is the second fastest 10 and under for the breaststroke in the history of U.S. Nationals. We also had a relay team that set a national record for relays. The team that beat that record was from north Baltimore and, I believe, had Michael Phelps on the team. So we were achievers. This program had become a place for people who wanted to achieve, to swim at the highest level.

As a result, we also began to have a larger contingency of white families pursuing the team. So I had all these swimmers leaving white teams and coming to join PDR. I mean it was a phenomenal thing to have and I didn't plan on having it. But I took it and ran with it. I thought a lot of good things would come from it because diversity brings a lot of opportunities. Imagine you are a white person who has never been up close and personal with an African American. They see something on TV and they think that's it. Then there is an African American who has never been up close and personal with a white person. Never been in their home, never seen how they live, never ate the food that they eat. There are people who literally live like that. I didn't grow up like that. I was exposed to everything and anything. My dad made sure. He was in Europe during the war, where African Americans were treated a whole lot differently than they were in America. He brought that back from the war and put that sense of justice and equality in my head as a young man. I lived my life with a sense of wanting to know everyone, experience everything and respecting diversity. So I felt that this was a tremendous opportunity not only for black kids, but also for white kids to experience something different, to experience that diversity.

To me, the PDR teams stood for Philadelphia, for diversity, for education and for success. My kids were proud to be on our team. When they went to a swim meet and were competing against suburban teams, with their great uniforms, great pool and all these coaches, my kids felt just as empowered. My kids would listen to them talk, listen in the locker room and come back feeling good. They would say, "We got work done. We should beat them." So they were proud of their team. They were proud that PDR was in the house. They were proud to be a member of PDR; they wore their colors well. Because they knew they were getting the same thing as the suburban kids. That's when I knew I was a success.

I believe our other success as a team is that we were a positive part of people's lives. I always think that if someone involved in PDR Swimming was about to be "put under" for an operation, and was asked to think of some positive thing in his or her life, that person would say our program. And I know that's true because a lot of those kids who came along during that time frame, they are still friends with the kids they swam with on the team. They are out, they are working, but they still get together at certain times of the year, share what they are doing. I don't care if they are in opposite ends of the country. They still connect with each other. The PDR team taught people how to swim, how to enjoy the sport, how to achieve in the sport at a very high level and to continue to swim. And even if they are not swimming, they are doing triathlons, biathlons. They're active. They're healthy. We developed some healthy minds. We develop positive young people who contribute to society. That's being successful. And we broke down stereotypes and myths that were in the country that African Americans can't swim. That was successful.

I tell people, whether you want to believe it or not, I think this was my calling. This is what I was meant to do. Starting the team and moving through all the trials and tribulations was not difficult for me. It was easy. It was like I had read it and I had been there before. It felt like something I just knew how to create. You set the team up. You have to ask people questions, but I asked the right questions. And I did mostly all the right things in getting it organized. I wanted these kids to have a smile on their face but also to learn things through swimming, to make them a little better prepared for what is coming in life. It really was my calling.

JOE BANNER

"I think we can try to use sports teams to reflect the values and attitudes about what kind of rights and obligations we have as citizens."

Growing up, I played every sport.

Sports were huge in Brookline, the most immediate suburb west of Boston where I grew up. I still have tons of memories to this day, maybe more then my limited on-field career warrants. I remember playing football with my friends. Playing little league in the community. Basketball games where I had to hit the first of a one and one, but missed it.

When I was a kid, I don't think I did anything but play sports. If my parents really made me, I'd study, but only for a little bit. I was always playing, whether it was just out on the street in front of the house or on some organized team. If I wasn't playing, I was watching sports, rooting for sports. When I was a kid we had season tickets to the Bruins. My dad and I probably went to twenty games a year at least. In fact, I got the love of sports from my parents. My dad was a solid athlete and my mom was a club champion in golf, as well as an accomplished tennis player. They would always come and watch me play, whether it was little league or school sports.

While sports had a big impact on me growing up, maybe the most influential experiences of my life were volunteering at a community center and going to a sleep-away camp as a kid. My volunteer work started when I switched schools. After going to public school my whole life, I switched to a private school called Rivers in 7th grade. They had a program on Fridays where a group of us would pile into a van and be driven to this community center where we would work with different kids. The goal was to both mentor and tutor them. With some of them, you would end up practicing reading or math, with others you would end up shooting baskets.

It was probably the first experience I had that allowed me to see and understand how different some people's lives were from my own, to have the feeling of helping somebody. People don't fully get it until they go and help somebody. It was a nice thing to experience at an early stage of my life. I was very touched by that and to this day my life is affected by that experience. And once I started better understanding how lucky I was, I felt I had to try and educate the school and the community about their obligation to try and make a difference in other peoples' lives.

So I wanted to try to put myself in a position to help other kids gain this understanding. When I was eight years old, I had gone to a sleep-away camp for two months. When you go to camp, you develop a certain degree of self-confidence and independence as well as an ability to get along with people. Since going to camp had been so powerful in my life, I began to think that giving that opportunity to others would lay a good foundation for their lives as well.

That's when I decided to start Camp E.

Camp E stood for camp and for education. We wanted to raise money to educate the kids at Rivers about the other side of the world, the part of the world that they weren't really experiencing. To get it started we had a bunch of typical high school fundraisers. We then used the money to send kids to camp on scholarships and to run programs, like bringing guests to speak about some of the problems of less fortunate people.

I enjoyed experiences like this so much that I continued on this path through college. In my senior year at Denison, I participated in a program called an urban semester, where a group of students were given an internship to work in the inner city. The goal was to give you an experience about a side of the world you weren't necessarily growing up in.

Ironically, it was this experience that led me back to sports. Through the urban semester program, I was able to get an internship at Philadelphia's WCAU, which did a lot of sports broadcasting. At the end of that internship I had one semester left in college, but they offered me a job. At that point to be in that big a market at that big a station at that age was significant, so I didn't want to pass that up.

I went back to Denison and made arrangements to complete my courses without actually going back to school. At that time, it was the U.S. Bicentennial, so all of the championships in the different sports and all-star games were in Philadelphia as part of the Bicentennial celebration. As part of my job I was assigned to covering all those events. I was also in the locker room when the Flyers won the Stanley Cup. It was pretty cool.

While I enjoyed doing that, I knew I wanted to start a non-profit. I had a degree in business, and enjoyed the idea of starting something from scratch. At the time, however, my friend of fifteen years, Jeffery Lurie, called and said he was trying to buy an NFL franchise. He asked if I wanted to be involved. It didn't take long to answer that question. We tried to buy the Patriots first, but that fell through, which was very disappointing. I didn't know if Jeff would give up, but he quickly decided to try again.

That was when the Eagles came into play.

We were in New York working with the lawyers, negotiating everything. And frankly, until we actually signed the papers, you just kept wondering whether it was going to happen or not. It was a very difficult negotiation. It went back and forth between looking hopeful and not looking hopeful. So when we finally signed the papers and it was official, it was very exciting.

Working for the Eagles has been a phenomenal experience. I am one of the only people whose job is the answer to "If you could have any job in the world, what would it be?" I look at my job as a jigsaw puzzle, as trying to figure out how to put together all the pieces for both the football team and the business operation, how to foster the integration of an incredibly diverse group of working people towards the same goals. My best memory is standing on the podium when we won the championship game, knowing we were going to the Super Bowl. I remember that feeling of not just mental but physical euphoria. I don't know what else there is in life that provides even the possibility of having that feeling.

In the midst of my work with the Eagles, however, I still wanted to be involved in helping the community. That is why I got involved with City Year, a program where 17-24 year olds provide critically

needed services to some of Philadelphia's most underserved children and young adults. After I got to really understand City Year, I actually thought it would benefit any city, especially Philadelphia. That is why I worked so hard, along with others, to get City Year into our city, and later, to focus on high school drop-outs.

We are talking about a city with a school district that is large, challenged and under-funded. We have a social responsibility to these students to make sure they get educated properly, so that at some point we can turn their lives over to them and say, you are responsible. But I don't think we really have the right as adults to do that until we have done everything we can to assure them that we have given all of them an equal chance by giving them a good education. So for me, the idea of taking City Year Corps members who are really young idealists wanting to make a difference in the world, and putting them together with young students, who in many cases want to do well but don't have the resources to do well, is a win-win. We can help the young people who are trying to tutor and mentor, we can help the school district that is overburdened and understaffed and we can do something for the Corps members that can change their lives and hopefully their perspective about what they want to do with the rest of their lives.

I have also tried to intertwine my passion for community service with the Eagles. The Eagles support and sponsor a City Year team. In addition, though, the Eagles have made the choice of having community service, education and the health of young people in the city a major focus of our organization. The Eagles Youth Partnership was the first and may still be the only non-profit affiliated with a sports team that does its own programming. You know, with most sports teams, you can send in an application to their foundation for a grant, for a thousand dollars or five thousand dollars, or whatever it may be, and they have people review the grants and give away some money. We do that, but in addition to that we created an impactful program to really make a difference in people's lives that we run ourselves.

When we were working on getting a stadium deal, Ed Rendell used to say that in Philadelphia he could walk down Market Street, see a person who is homeless, then see a person dressed up in a fancy suit walking into an office building, and know that there is only one thing about which they could probably have enough in common to have a dialogue: their favorite sports team. Especially if it was the morning after a big win. So sports has that unique power of being something that brings people together towards a commonality to which they have so much passion, and then it becomes this powerful shared experience within a family, a small little community or a whole city. So when you have something that becomes that powerful, that so many people share, it becomes something larger that can bring people together.

I like the idea of using the sense of community generated by sports teams, such as the Eagles, to model for individuals and other corporations how to come together and fulfill a larger social responsibility to our city. With the Eagles Youth Foundation and City Year, which for me is my personal, primary execution of my own sense of social responsibility, I think we can try to use sports teams to reflect the values and attitudes about what kind of rights and obligations we have as citizens.

I guess I still feel the need to try to persuade people about their obligation to try and make a difference in other peoples' lives.

DANIEL DIAZ

"There were 'A' students, 'corner' kids, kids who had never played before but just wanted the chance. They all came to play and gave it their all. It was amazing, it was a great season."

I wasn't a bad kid, but I wasn't a good kid, either.

I had a couple friends who were in small-time gangs and also some who got into selling drugs. I wasn't going to stop hanging with them, though. They were my friends. I was a man capable of choosing to do the right or wrong thing, but sometimes I would follow them and get myself into some trouble. I was going the wrong way.

I was also in danger of dropping out of school. I had stopped going to some of my classes. I didn't like the environment. I thought that the teacher was too busy scolding the kids. She seemed to spend more time trying to get them to pay attention than being concerned about me learning anything. I felt I was wasting my time being taught stuff that I had already learned. So I got into trouble and, eventually, I was asked to be transferred out of school.

Then when I was 17, my daughter came along. I thought to myself, this is amazing. I had never seen anything like this before. I didn't know if I should jump for joy or pass out. I knew this changed everything. From that moment on I got focused. I finally started to listen. I heard about a school called Community Academy of Philadelphia that gave young parents another chance, and I enrolled. So during this time, I would go home, eat, get my books out and that would be it. After working hard, I graduated with honors. Then I started to work for the Lighthouse, a community center in Kensington.

This is where my drive to get the kids moving in the right direction, get them doing something positive in the neighborhood, comes from. This is why my brother and I started the football league in North Philadelphia.

When we first started, I would just get in my car, grab a bunch of flyers and go to the kids playing in the streets and in the schoolyards. We passed out about one hundred and sixty flyers the first year and over seventy kids showed up. We were only supposed to keep twenty-two kids. That's when my younger brother, Andy, said, "Why don't we start to have age brackets? Let more kids play." The next year, we doubled our numbers to over one hundred and forty. Two years later, we had two hundred and twenty kids show up. The lines were all the way from the field to the street. There were kids from all places and nationalities—Asian, African American, White, Hispanic, Dominican and Nigerian. There were even a couple of Arabian kids. These kids did awesome. There were "A" students, "corner" kids, kids who had never played before but just wanted the chance. They all came to play and gave it their all. It was amazing, it was a great season.

After my first year, I had a bunch of parents come to me and tell me that I must do this every year. I understood. And I did because I had always felt that I could talk to my coaches about the things I couldn't talk to my parents about. My coaches always showed us love and made sure we were doing the right thing. That is why I am here now and why we see ourselves as mentors to the kids. There are plenty of times that we take care of the kids. If they can't afford league fees or if they need cleats or even if they don't want to get up for school, we are the ones to go to their houses and wake them up. We're the ones who go to the school if they're suspended because the parents don't have a car. I've received all types of phone calls. I just got one where a kid was stabbed and the mom called me to give her a ride to the hospital because she didn't have a car. Last year, I had three kids from "the corners" on my team. I had to literally go to those corners and pick them up. A couple times they told me they couldn't come because they were going to make some money. I told them I would pay them whatever they thought they were going make just as long as they got their butts on that field.

I do all this because by playing football with us for a few hours, the kids learn more than the game and stay out of trouble for a few hours. The kids learn healthy habits, and it helps build character and self-esteem. A lot of these kids come in here with their heads always down, not talking, not sure about themselves. Some of them come in with really nasty attitudes they learned from the streets. You see something constantly, it is going to rub off on you. A lot of times these kids are doing and saying things only to be cool with other kids. They come in and call out "Yo" or "Hey man." I just tell them "I'm the coach. This is how you talk to me. This is how we are going talk to one another, this is how you are going to behave, or you're not going to play." Last year, there were about 240 players. Towards the end of the season, we only had about 170 players because the kids are not allowed to fight, curse, be late or miss a certain number of practices. If they did, we have to let them go. But if they stay, the kids learn a lot from football. Their school grades come up. Behavior changes. Some stop running the streets. Some start coaching, and some take the skills to the next level at school and higher.

There was one kid, for instance, who came from a troubled neighborhood. He had great parents, but always had his head down. He got traded from team to team. No coach wanted to deal with him. Finally, I put him on my team. Now he shows up everyday, works hard, has two jobs at the Lighthouse, really keeping busy. He was just hanging out with the wrong crowd. I showed him that I knew the kinds of guys he was hanging out with. I said, "You can listen to them if you want to go that way. I had friends like that, too, at one point in my life, but I was not going to have those people hold me back." That's what I teach: Don't let anyone hold you back. Now he's straightened out a lot. He comes home, does his work, shows up to practice. He lost a lot of weight, too. He came to me at 270 and now he is down to 175. He just kept that workout even after he stopped playing for us. He's getting ready to graduate on time. He's thinking college. As long as he graduates, I know I was a benefit in his life.

It's like Johnny Irizarry. He was like a coach to me. He taught me to know what you want before you do it, to take on only what you can handle, to be a hundred and ten percent at everything you choose to do. Everything he has done and shown me has taught me and benefited me. He is a positive role model. He's helped us out a lot. He gave us the fields for the league. Then he gave us grant money to help the league grow. He got me to work for the Lighthouse for a second time. I'm glad that I have him in my life. He is a great guy. I am so proud of him being named to the Philadelphia Public School Reform Commission. I went to his inauguration; it was a good thing to see him up there. I would like to be like Johnny. He is my favorite Latino community leader.

I coached for four seasons for The Lighthouse, two teams per season, won two championships both undefeated with two totally different groups of kids and called it quits. Basically I have retired from coaching and spend all my time with my kids. They kept saying that I was spending too much time on the football field. I thought if these guys are telling me that, then I better call it quits. I see my role as a father, almost like I see my role as a coach. It's to provide moral support, to teach them to go the right way with their lives. I think I have been doing a very good job of that, no problems in school. And I think that by keeping them busy, involved in martial arts and sports, is helping me out. The best part about being a dad and a coach is being with them, going to the practice, going to the games, being there when they need you.

My whole family, kids and all—Mom, Dad, sisters, and bros—were all there when we won the two football championships. We had named the championship trophy after Juan Alicea, a good friend of mine. He was basically like my cousin. We started a football team with him awhile back. He was going to move in with me because he was having some trouble. He went to a club one night and stopped to make a phone call. While he was sitting there, some guys came up, thought that he was someone else and shot him. The news got back, and I had to break the news to everyone. Everyone in the neighborhood knew who he was. The league was just getting started a few years later, and my brother came up with the idea of getting a full-sized picture of Juan and a trophy to name after Juan. After the first championship game, the trophy was given to Juan's parent by the winning coach. We wanted to remind people that when you want to do something in life and you keep getting pulled away into others things like Juan did things like that may happen. We felt by putting that message out there, and jamming that football into their faces all the time, we could save a lot of kids. And I think we did.

FRANK GRECO

"I think now there's a culture and attitude that, you know, we're going to win. We're going to play hard, we come to practice, no BS. My players are convinced that they're better prepared than the opponents because they work harder. And they love the game."

In many ways, I grew up at Max Myers playground in Northeast Philadelphia.

There were a million kids in the neighborhood and they were always at the playground. It was not out of the ordinary for us to get ten, twelve kids, go to the playground, and play six-on-six, or seven-on-seven baseball games.

In the summer, all I did was play ball from sunup to sundown. We used to play box ball, or half ball, wire ball, step ball—that's what we did. Day in and day out, in the street or at the playground.

Back then none of us had a ton of money. It was like, well gee, who has a ball? So we used to open the sewer tops, and with a wire hanger, we'd make a loop and fish balls out of the sewer. Or somebody would take their mother's mop handle and that'd be the half ball stick, until they got in trouble. Then it was somebody else's turn to get the mop handle the next time. But we literally had a ball in our hands ten, twelve hours a day, every single day. Even in the snow, we'd play football in the street. Softball and basketball, that was at the playground. But a lot of the stuff we just played in the street. We'd get some chalk, make bases, and off we went. Way different nowadays.

Nowadays, it's rare that you could find eight kids and go play four on four at a playground. It's just rare. Now everything is organized. You belong to this association, and your practice is at this time. Rarely can you show up at a playground and play ball. I mean in the old days, you just went, and whoever was there, you just kind of blended in and played. Now you'd have to make ten phone calls to see if you had guys that are willing to go to the playground, see if their parents can drive them to the playground, so you could play some type of pick-up game or something along those lines.

Central High School was also different back then. I graduated from Central High School with the 228th graduating class in 1969. At the time, it was an all-boys school; that made it different. I mean the girls that are here are tremendous. Bright, articulate, athletic. Just great. It's been a wonderful boon for Central High School to have the girls. But it was different back then when it was just guys. When it's all boys, it's all locker room humor, all the time. When it's co-ed, for the most part, guys watch their p's and q's. It's been a wonderful boon for Central High School to have the girls.

Still, coming out of high school, I wasn't sure what I was going to do. My parents were divorced and my mother was a seamstress, so I didn't have a lot of money. I got into Penn State Abington through the help of a counselor here named Bill Disharoon, who was here for like 60 years. Best man ever. I thought I was going to be a plumber, but he said, "Come here." He made a phone call and said, "Go see this person." I went over to the Abington campus, brought the paperwork, and they looked at it, and said, "Okay, you come in the fall."

I played basketball in college for two years, very successful—it was a great time. But my grades were shaky. Since I was still at home, I was hanging out on the weekends and running around with my friends. My grades were borderline, but still good enough that I got to transfer to the main campus. Once I got there, I ended up being on Dean's List five out of the six trimesters. So I managed to get stuff together. I was away from home and had three roommates who were pretty studious. I mean, we had fun, but there was a lot of time to study. So I did very well.

At one point, I decided I wanted to be a doctor. I started to take pre-med courses, but when I wasn't studying or in class, I was always outside, playing ball or some sport. My love for sports made me realize that I didn't have it in me to be a doctor. I didn't have what it would take to do four years of college, four years of med school, internship, etc. So I made the call, I went to my mother, and I told her I didn't want to be a doctor anymore. She was very upset; she always wanted a doctor. And I probably had the brains to be a doctor, but it wasn't what I wanted to do. I wanted to coach and be around sports. Dress in gym clothes at work, you know?

I thought I'd be a gym teacher. I figured it'd be a lot of fun. The teachers that I had at Central were always pretty good guys. They seemed to have a good time. So I went that route, got my teaching degree, and next thing I knew, I had my first job at Stetson Longfellow Annex. I bounced around before I finally ended up at my alma mater, Central High School.

Back then, getting a head-coaching job at a high school was difficult. Someone usually had to die in order for you to get it. I was an assistant to the head coach here at Central, but when he got sick, I was able to take over. I was very lucky to get a head coaching position so quickly. I coached the boys for about thirteen years.

And then my daughter made the girls basketball team as a freshman.

The head coach had just retired, and my daughter kind of suggested I try to be the coach of her team. So on the last possible day, I decided that it would be a pretty neat thing to coach my daughter. I gave up the boys' job, and I became the girls' coach.

I did it because I have a very intact ego. I know I can coach. Some people said, "Oh, you're going to go steal money. Coaching the girls, it's not really basketball." And I said, "No, I intend to coach them just like the boys. They're athletes. We're going to play a full schedule. We're going to go play good teams. If we lose, we lose, but we're going to get after it." So with that attitude, I moved over to the girls and the run that we've had has been incredible.

It seems everybody loves to talk about the streak of winning 101 public league games in a row. But the truth is, I didn't realize we had the streak going for a long time. We were playing seventeen, eighteen games a year. So the first three, four years, it didn't even click. Then somebody pointed out to me that we had won like fifty or sixty straight games.

How did we do it? I don't have an answer for it because there are some great teams in the public league. We had a handful of games that could have gone either way. It's hard to put into words. I mean, how do you explain that you went 101 games without losing? I mean that's like seven years and change, winning every league game and playoffs.

The best way I can explain it is we got there the same way you get anywhere in life: we worked. I mean, we practiced every day, two hours or more every day. There might only be two or three days in a year, from late October to March, when we didn't practice. And that's tough for everybody. For the kids, that's a pounding on their legs. But we've never had the problem of kids not wanting to come to practice—and that's a testament to the players and the school.

We also played as a team. Our roster top to bottom was filled with unbelievably talented kids. We played shift basketball because we had such good talent—it was ridiculous to have such talented kids sit on the bench. So what we did is we said, "Okay, every four minutes we're putting another five in," which was radical for high school basketball. First of all, most high schools don't have five good players. But our starters bought into it. They'd sit down, the next group would go in there, and we'd press everybody. Didn't make a difference who you were, we pressed you from baseline to baseline, and we ran the ball down your throat. By the middle of the third quarter, every team we played was exhausted. But we were still running kids in who had lots of energy because they're playing half a game.

My role as coach is not just to teach them the game, but to really be their coach. And that is one thing I love about my job. An English teacher sees his kids for fifty minutes a day. But during that fifty minutes, depending on the lesson, the teacher might talk to none of the kids or might talk to half a dozen kids. In basketball, this year I think we had thirteen or fourteen kids on the team. I get to talk to every one of them every day for two hours for five months. I get to know who's working, who's not working, who's got problems here, and who's got academic issues there, who's got detention. I get a chance to talk to them every single day. And the camaraderie that the girls themselves establish by being together is different than in any type of other setting.

Sports also teaches you how to deal with winning and losing. If you lose a tough game, you got to come back and practice on Monday, then again on Tuesday, and play Wednesday. You got to learn how to shake that off and come back and get ready for the next game. You can't get into a depression where you're useless for a week. That doesn't do anybody any good. I'll give you a quick example. We played Chester. We went down 20, came back to go up 1. We made up the 20 points in the last quarter, in 8 minutes. We were down 20, came back, go up 1, with like 30 seconds to go. We get fouled. If we make the one-on-one, we're winning the game. The girl misses the front end of one-on-one. Chester scores with four seconds to go. We lose by one.

That's a crushing defeat. My position in the locker room is, "What a great game you guys played. You showed a lot of heart." I didn't go into the locker room and yell my head off. Then we came back to school on Monday, and practiced Monday. Practiced Tuesday. Played on Wednesday. Won on Wednesday. And we moved on. It really does teach character, you know. You have to learn how to deal with the good and the bad.

A guy named Fred Shero coached the Flyers, and when they won the first Stanley Cup, the thing he put on the board before the game was "Win today and we will walk together forever." I tell the kids that before every championship. Every championship. I tell them that because it's true. No matter what championship it is, the first or the ninth, it's theirs. There were kids this year who were involved in their first championship in which they were major participants. Ten years from now, God willing I'm around, I'll cross paths with the kids, and they'll say, "Hey, remember when we beat…" You know what I'm saying? So there's a very special camaraderie that coaches build up with kids that teachers can't, just by the nature of the classroom structure. And that's what separates us.

Through the years and the streak, the players changed, but the attitude never did. I think now there's a culture and attitude that, you know, we're going to win. We're going to play hard. We come to practice, no BS. My players are convinced that they're better prepared than the opponents because they work harder. And they love the game.

That is what got me to where I am today. I followed what I loved. Could I have made more money as a doctor? Absolutely. But I'm back at my alma mater. I'll never be a millionaire, but that's okay. You know, I like to think that I had some influence or impact on young kids, and that's a good thing to take with me.

WIN

DAN TERSTEIN

"My most important role as Commissioner, though, was to make sure the league kept the importance it holds in the community. And to understand that importance, it helps to understand Mt. Airy."

I remember the moment when I decided that I needed to become the Commissioner of the Mt Airy Baseball League. I was watching a player getting ready to catch a fly ball. He missed it, but then picked up the ball and threw it to his teammate in left field…who threw it back to him.

The coach at the time, who was a wonderful guy and was super supportive, ran up to the player and said, "That's the best throw I've ever seen." I remember thinking that we can't do it like this anymore. We need to teach them how to do this the right way or not at all. So I volunteered to be the Commissioner.

I first started coaching in the Mt Airy League when my oldest son, Jacob, was 5. He is 23 now, so about 18 years ago. I started by coaching tee ball, and it was a lot of fun. He kept playing, so I kept coaching. I was the assistant coach of his team until he was 10 or 11, and then I started to get involved with Micah's team, my other son.

The league at that time was not a competitive league. There were roughly two groups of parents. One group would always ask why we had to keep score. The other group was extremely competitive, win-at-all-costs. It seemed like they would rip your heart out to win a ball game. That the two groups coexisted so well was pretty miraculous, but the level of play often wasn't all that good. There was no drafting of players based on ability at the time, so there were some horrible mismatches.

When I became the Commissioner, the biggest change that first year was instituting a draft to balance out the players' abilities. The draft was traumatic for some folks who had been with the league for a long time. The "it's only a game, non-score keepers" were used to being together. The parents of the more skilled, more competitive kids were

afraid that their kids were going to have to play with kids who didn't know what hand the glove goes on. There were some intense meetings where people would say thing like "my child's identity is as a Cub" or "that is the way things have always been, why change?" It was a difficult transition, to assess and assign kids based on ability instead of letting a coach load up on the best players. That was the beginning.

While teaching kids to play baseball is the part I enjoy the most, my most important role as Commissioner over the years has been to make sure the league kept the importance it holds in the community. And to understand that importance, it helps to understand Mt. Airy.

Mt. Airy is an interesting and sometimes complex place. The neighborhood changed less than some in the 60's and 70's, when the entire city was transitioning. Realtors were scaring people into selling their homes out of the fear that Blacks were going to move in and change their lives. In some communities, for sale signs would go up immediately and whole neighborhoods would change almost overnight. It is striking how the city's demographics changed in a short period of time.

Unlike other parts of the city, most white families stayed and Mt. Airy remained relatively stable and fully integrated. It has become one of the most racially diverse communities in the country. The neighborhood is diverse, not only racially, but economically and socially. However, the integration of the sports leagues, like other community institutions in Mt Airy, has not always been as successful. There is a football team that plays on the same field as we do that is 99% black, and the basketball league is overwhelmingly black as well. The closest neighborhood school is 98% black.

But the baseball league has always managed to reflect the neighborhood it plays in.

I can't explain why this is the case. It was a culture that existed before I got there and has been maintained. After being part of it for so many years, it is easy to take it for granted, but in looking at the re-segregation of so many institutions in one of the most integrated communities in the country, I'm reminded that we have something special.

I've never counted the hours I spend a week helping the league continue on, nor do I want to. I know it is a lot. But it's not something I do by myself. Part of what has made the league work is that there is a core of 6-8 folks that that have been doing it longer than I have. I couldn't do it without them and the hundreds of volunteers who coach, work the concession stand and maintain the fields.

The challenge was bringing the two groups together—the competitive ones with the non-competitive ones—and making them both understand what they could learn from each other. One group needed to learn that baseball is a competition and games should be competitive. The other group needed to learn that we don't measure success by the number of games we win. Youth sports need to be instructional above all and kids need to feel like they are learning. Losing and making mistakes are part of the game, but it's important to learn something from the experience. I suppose it comes back to that moment when the kids were in the outfield throwing the ball to one another, having a great time, but not learning anything about the game. They already loved the game. They needed to learn how to play.

A lot has changed since then. The league has doubled in size. We now have kids who improve every year because of the work of some wonderful coaches. The games are usually close. The kids love to win, but learn from losing. About 40 kids each year go on to play for their high school teams. Eight or nine go on to play college baseball, and we've had three players taken in the Major League Draft in the last five years. The league has become a real baseball league, but without losing the special place it holds in our neighborhood.

While it's been great to see the success the kids have had on the baseball field, overall, I see it mostly as a community-building activity. I believe the League has an important place in my community. It is part of how we become connected to one other. Parents coach the kids of other parents. A family brings a snack every week. Each family takes a turn working at the concession stand. It's a community league.

One story that sticks out in my mind is a time I was hanging by the snack stand, talking to a mother, and she's telling me how she feels about the changes in the league over the years, and what an event the games have become in the community. I said something about how special the League is and how we sometimes take the League for granted. She said, "Oh, no, I never take it for granted; it has helped me raise my kids."

I thought that was a profound statement and very true for many of us. As the kids reflect back on it, I hope they will remember that they came to know people from different cultures and backgrounds that they would not have met otherwise. They will have met an incredible cast of characters and hopefully learned something from some of them. They will have learned about winning and losing and trying again. I do think it has helped all of us raise our kids. Not that any of us should claim responsibility for raising another person's child, but that is in a way what happens out there.

In any event, I think we are all better people for having been a part of it. I know I am.

JESSE BIDDLE

Mt.Airy Baseball Player,
Philadelphia Phillies No.1 Draft Choice

Getting drafted by the Phillies, my home team, in the first round was unlike any moment I've ever had. It was just phenomenal. It was something I had been waiting a long time for. It was a dream of mine. Not a lot of people get to realize their dream. I did.

I know that none of this would have been possible without Mt. Airy Baseball. I still remember to this day being eleven years old and scoring the winning run in the championship game. My whole team piled on top of me. You play for those moments.

And the lessons I learned on Mt. Airy baseball fields are the ones I'll use for the rest of my life. I learned about competiveness, sportsmanship and how to handle adversity. It's when you deal with adversity that your true character shows. Everyone deals with adversity, but you have to bounce back and keep working hard. That's one of the reasons I was able to make it.

We value sports for many reasons: the goals, the mindset it gives you, the lessons you learn, how it brings people together. When parents see their kids playing sports, competing, trying their best, showing sportsmanship, they see how it brings out the best in their children.

Everyone understands the value of sports on some level.

It's the universal language.

SONNY HILL

"I've seen too many situations where basketball players were outstanding in their period, but they didn't maximize it because they didn't understand the importance of education. Education gives you the opportunity to get to where you want to go over the long period."

Whatever it is that I've done in my life has all come out of what my grandmother, Matty N. Terry, and, my grandfather, Lottie Brown, instilled in me. And when I think about what they were able to do for me, I have to then go back to my great-grandfather and my great-grandmother on my mother's side. They all taught me the basics, the things that would help me as I moved along in society. They didn't see it from that point of view. It was just the way that people were raised from generation to generation, but it gave me a base that allowed me to become who I am.

Now with all that being said, what is that really all about? Well, it's really about knowing how to interact with people for the right reason. Within my culture and my time of growing up, Philadelphia in the 1930's and 40's, it was learning how to say "Please," how to say "Thank you" and how to put a handle on somebody's name by calling them "Mister" or "Miss." It was about how to respect people across the board and to have those people take you under their wing. A lot of time people don't understand that when children are being raised, they are not only raised by the people in their immediate household; they are also raised by the people surrounding that household, whether they are aunts and uncles, nephews and cousins, extended family, or just people in the community. I was fortunate enough to have all of that as part of my upbringing. So that helped me formulate, early on, who I was going to be and how I was going to move forward into society at that time.

Most people know my background because it's entrenched in basketball. Baseball, though, was my first love. When I was growing up basketball was just a blip on the radar screen. Football wasn't really that big. There were only two sports that were really dominant in America. One was boxing and the other was baseball. I was an outstanding baseball player. Baseball helped me to begin to open doors that Negroes and colords of my era had not gone through previously. For instance, I was very fortunate that when I was in the ninth grade of Gillespie Junior High School, I was one of four Negroes to make the Walpert Post Baseball Team, managed by Joe Ercolani and located at the Nicetown's Boys and Girls Club. We were the first blacks to break the color line in American Legion baseball. Of course, at the time you don't really pay attention to that fact. You know what's going on, but you don't really pay attention to it.

Because I played baseball for Walpert Post, I had a baseball uniform, and it made me somewhat of an idol, someone that my community looked up to. When I left my home, I had my baseball uniform on. When I went to play baseball, I had my baseball uniform. And when I came back from baseball, I had my baseball uniform on. So the community that I lived in at 2327 North 16th Street identified with me from that point of view. But whatever I had, I was willing to share with my friends, the people I grew up with. It was how I was raised. It's always been a part of me. And in most cases, I had more than the people I grew up with because the grandmother, who raised me, always provided the best. From that point, I had a lot to share. So if I had a wagon, they had a wagon. If I had a bike, they had a bike. If I had toys, they had toys. I was willing to share because that's basically my nature, how I was raised. As I moved on with my life, I've tried to be more of a giver than a receiver.

The guys in my neighborhood played baseball, but they didn't play American Legion baseball. They didn't have a team. So I was the guy that they looked up to, and I helped form a baseball team in my neighborhood called the 16th Street Cardinals. And who was the leader of 16th Street Cardinals? Who was the guy that did all the things that needed to be done? I was. So as I went on in my life-that willingness to share and help build opportunities for others became a trend over the many years of my life. But I didn't know it at that point in my life. I was just Sonny Hill. I was a good baseball player. I played American Legion baseball. I had an identity. I had to use that identity to share the opportunity of playing baseball. I felt people relied on me, looked up to me and revered me for that willingness and need to share opportunities with others.

When I made the transition into basketball, I was playing at a place called Fun Field, but that's now called Cecil B. Moore. We used to take our group from 16th Street, which was not a basketball group, and go up there and play. In their community, they played basketball, so they were better than we were. When I first started going to Fun Field, I wasn't even good enough to play at the little end, where the younger guys like me played. I couldn't even get in those games. I had to get winners. But I worked hard. I learned my skill. Eventually, I was good enough to be chosen in the younger guy games. The big thing, though, was to start to play with the older guys who were playing down at the big end. The goal was to be asked to play with them when they didn't have enough players. And one day they said, "Yo, you, come up here and play." I couldn't believe it. Of course, when you first play with the older guys, you just fit in. Pass the ball. Move the ball out. Do whatever. And then it transitions and they say, "Shoot the ball." And when they said that to me, I couldn't believe it. "What? The older guys telling me to shoot the ball?" And that's when they began to take me under their wing and teach me and help me to become even more secure and confident in what I was doing in basketball.

One day I was playing basketball at Fun Field and Guy Rodgers tapped me. He said, "Man, you can play." Well, Guy was like everything in the community. ,He was my mentor and my hero. For him to say that I could play just sent a message, and we became very, very close. He's my big brother; I'm his little brother. That's the way we refer to one another. So I started to identify with him. I used to go with him to play. I listened to what he was saying. I learned the game. I learned to be a competitor. I learned to play hard. I learned to do things the way that he did them, which in turn helped me become a better basketball player.

As I became a better basketball player, I had to decide whether I was going to continue to play baseball or whether I was going to continue to play basketball. When I went to Northeast High School, I went there to play baseball. Even though Guy was my hero and I followed him in basketball, I knew what I could do in baseball. So I was confident about that. Baseball was still the sport that I loved the most, but I was getting better in basketball. As I made the transition, I found out that by putting more priority in basketball, I began to become a better basketball player. I could jump. I could dunk the ball. I could play above the rim. I could shoot jump shots. I could stop on a dime. I was becoming a pretty well known basketball player.

In 10th grade, I played on the junior varsity basketball team which was a big thing. I was like the sixth or seventh man on the junior varsity. My junior year in high school I tried out for and made varsity. Not only did I make the team, my coach, Ike Wooley, another important person in my life, picked me to start. And as a senior, I was the co-captain with T. Parham, who is regarded as the greatest schoolyard basketball player that this city has ever developed. T. Parham was the man. He was all that and then some. We had known one another since we were fourteen years old because we played on the Zion Stars, the junior team of Dr. Leon Sullivan's church. In fact, I remember Coach Wooley saying something to me in high school that I didn't understand until much, much later. He said to me, "Sonny, it's a shame that you're here at the same time that T. is here." And it never dawned on me that what he was saying was that T. was good in high school, but he understood what my work ethic was and my drive.

See, I have a work ethic and a drive that is second to none. And I think that comes from my background and my family. I've always wanted to succeed. Now I was never really accepted as the premiere, prime time player, but the reality was none of them, except for Guy Rogers, were able to go where I went when playing basketball. I think a lot of that was the work ethic, a lot of that was the drive, a lot of that was determination, a lot of that was playing outside my community, interacting with other people, knowing how to deal with people and how to play in different environments. So Coach Wooley saw the qualities in me and, like all these other individuals, he almost predicted where I would be as my life went on. I had no idea because I was just doing what I needed to do.

Here is where Bob Custer becomes important in my life. While I was playing basketball at Northeast High School, I also used to carry Guy Roger's gym bag when he went to play games for an independent team coached by Custer. Now I was proud to go with Guy Rogers and carry his bag, but I didn't play in the games. I sat at the end of the bench in my street clothes. When the game was over, he'd go downstairs, take a shower, get his stuff, and I'd put it in the bag and then we would leave. Well, through that, Custer recognized me. So when Guy went to college at Temple University, and I was in 11th grade, Custer came to see me at my grandmother's house. He said to me, "I want you to play with my team." He had different names for the team, but one of the names of the team was Cozy Morely, one of the great comedians this area has ever seen. So I said, "Okay, what do I have to do?" Then my grandmother stepped in and said, "Well, if he's going to play for you, tell me what *you're* going to do." Custer said, "I'm going to pick him up. We're going to play. And I'm going to bring him back." With that answer, my grandmother let me play. But beyond putting me on his team, Custer also gave me an opportunity to get money to play basketball. I received five dollars a game.

Now I could play. But I didn't realize at that point how good I was as a player because in my basketball career, as I said, I grew up playing with T. Parnham and T. was better than I was in high school. Custer's other players would tell me how good I was as a player, but I'd say, "I'm good, but I'm not better than T." So basically I've tried not to ever get caught up in me. It's just about what I do. But when I was playing with them, I was basically being paid to score thirty to fifty-five points a game. I mean, when I had less than thirty points, it was a bad game. And I had a lot of games that were thirty to fifty-five. The key was, in that system, if you could play, they'd lay the ball right on you. So I had a guy by the name of Obie O'Brien from LaSalle High School, whose father was the legendary coach there, who would lay that ball right on me. There was another guy named Jim Maloney. He laid that ball right on me as well. So when I'd come off the screens, the ball was right there. Once I had the ball, I could do what needed to be done. I could score. That helped me confidence-wise. It helped me to show that I could play. And what it also did was show me that I could play basketball outside of my immediate community where a lot of my peers got caught. They were never ever able to play beyond their neighborhood.

By playing for Custer, I also moved beyond the Negro and colored community. Just like in American Legion baseball, I was the only black on an all-white team. I was only the second black to play basketball in what we now refer to as the Northeast, before it became the greater Northeast. Guy Rogers was the first. So you see how carrying Guy Roger's bag all comes back. And through that, I moved into another world that, unbeknownst to me, gave me an opportunity to expand my horizons. I was now interacting with people who in most cases rarely came in contact with Negroes or coloreds and vice-versa. I had the opportunity to do that. At those moments, I rarely ran across situations where there was bigotry. I'm not saying it wasn't there, but also I think a lot of it goes back to again to my upbringing. We were taught through my generation and my family to respect people. When I had to interact with people outside of my ethnic background, there was always that "Please" and "Thank you." Also, my grandmother who raised me always made sure that I dressed well. I mean, from a baby, you see any pictures of me back in the day I'm always dressed well. When I went to play, I was dressed well. Doesn't mean I had a shirt and tie on, but I was always well dressed. I think that sends a message. I've also always been basically well spoken. I've known how to interact with people and speak and do that kind of thing. And what that did was bridged the gap for me to interact with people from different social backgrounds, ethnic backgrounds and religious backgrounds.

As I graduated from high school, I got an opportunity to go to Center State College. Now in my household, we never had anyone even graduate high school. There was no discussion about education other than "You'd better go to school, boy." So I went to school every day, turned in all of my work, did all the things I needed to do. At that time, though, I was also playing for Pete Gillespie, who had a team called Hannibal AC. So one day, sitting on his step, he started to talk about education. He said, "You need to think about being in a situation where you can have courses that will allow you to go to college—academic courses." Originally, I was going to Northeast High School to be an auto mechanic. I listened to Gillespie, though, and changed my schedule from the industrial courses to the academic courses, the courses where you take the languages and the math that will prepare you for college. That put me in a position where, when I graduated from Northeast High School, I was ready for college. Of course, in most Negro or colored families, and even some white families, at that time, after you graduated from high school you got a job. But my grandmother, who worshipped me, allowed me to do something beyond simply get a job. She gave me the opportunity to do some things that I wanted to do. She allowed me to go to college and play basketball.

At that time, however, blacks didn't get the opportunity they have now to go to division one schools—even if you were a well known player such as myself. For instance, when I graduated, I was a very noted basketball player—a second team All Public, an outstanding independent and recreation leagues player. My basketball skills combined with my academic grades enabled me to be academically and athletically eligible for college. Yet, when I came out of high school, I think I may have had two offers to go to school. The Central State College offer was actually prompted by a gentleman named Bob Dabney, who worked for the Department of Recreation. He knew I could play basketball and his family lived on the campus of Central State College. So he arranged for me to get a grant-in-aid to go to there—they didn't have scholarships back in those days. The Central State coach had never even seen me play, but thanks to Bob Dabney, I was now on his team.

So I get on the train to go to Central State College, get off at this little town, Wilberforce, Ohio, and go to the campus. I'm there for a couple of days and before I even get over to the bursar to see about my grant-in-aid, the coach sees me. At that time, I'm five-nine, probably weigh a hundred and thirty-five pounds. I don't think I would've been impressed with me, either, even though I knew I had the ability to play and my scrapbook of clips was impressive. But of course, he had never seen me play. So he looked at me and said, "Well, I don't think we really have anything for you." I said "Well, if you don't have anything for me, I'm going to have to go back home." Meanwhile, I'd been playing over on the basketball court. Now I was ahead of my time when it came to basketball for my size. I mean, I could block shots on the backboard, which only Wilt Chamberlain was doing at that time. I could dunk a basketball. I could stop on a dime and shoot jump shots. I reeked confidence. I mean I'm talking the game. Well, word got back to the coach about how good I was as a player, and all of a sudden the coach has that grant-in-aid for me and I can stay in college.

So basketball practice starts. The coach had never started a freshman. I was good enough that it forced him to have to start me, but the coach resented that fact that he had to start me. In his tradition, he had never started a freshman. During our season, though, I helped to lead Central State to the District 22 NAIA Championship. We were also the first black school in the history of Ohio to go to and then to win the District 22 Championship, which gave us the opportunity to play in Kansas City for the NAIA tournament. I always tell people that the only two freshmen in the Mid-West Athletic Association that were All Conference their freshman year were Dick Barnett, who was on the New York Knicks championship team, and myself.

When the college year ended, I went home, but I didn't get a job. I called the coach and said "You know, coach, I'm coming back but I didn't get a job over the summer. Is there something I can get to be able to come back?" The coach didn't give me anything, though, so I stayed home the first part of the year. The team ended up having a bad season and the people in the school contacted me, saying, "Son, you gotta come back. You gotta do this. You gotta do that." So I go back the second half of the school year and play, but the tension was still there. When I came home after my second year of college, I had an opportunity to play in the Gold Medal basketball tournament, where all the best independent and college basketball players participated. I'm playing with Bob Custer's team again and I set a record by scoring fifty-five points in the tournament, while also averaging thirty-nine points a game.

So right after the tournament, I got a chance to try out for the Eastern Basketball League's Allentown Jets. Now of all the players I talked about so far, I'm the only one who made the team. So I chose playing for the league over returning to college. Now I had a relatively successful career in the Eastern Basketball League, but once again, I found myself breaking barriers. I was the first black on the Allentown Jet basketball team, and during that period, I ran across some racism and some problems, but you get to the point where you're still evolving in terms of who you are. You're more aware that you are breaking down barriers and that now the door becomes more open for others. And the people in that upstate Pennsylvania area loved me and still love me, whether it's in Allentown, Wilkes-Barre, Scranton, Sunberry, Hazelton or Williamsport. They all know me, know of me, and had great respect for me from that point of view.

Most of the things that I've done have really been done with my impetus, like the 16th Street Cardinals. And I've been fortunate enough that people think enough about me to just join in. It's almost like Sonny says we ought to do this and we're going to do it. We ended up with others who became a part of the cast, but I was always the one that set the tone for everything. When I helped form the Baker League in 1960, professional basketball players didn't have a place to play during the summer. So what we did back in the day was play pick-up games with players from different parts of the city. You had South Philadelphia, which had Sunny Lord and John Chaney. You had West Philadelphia, which had Hal Lear and Jay Norman. You

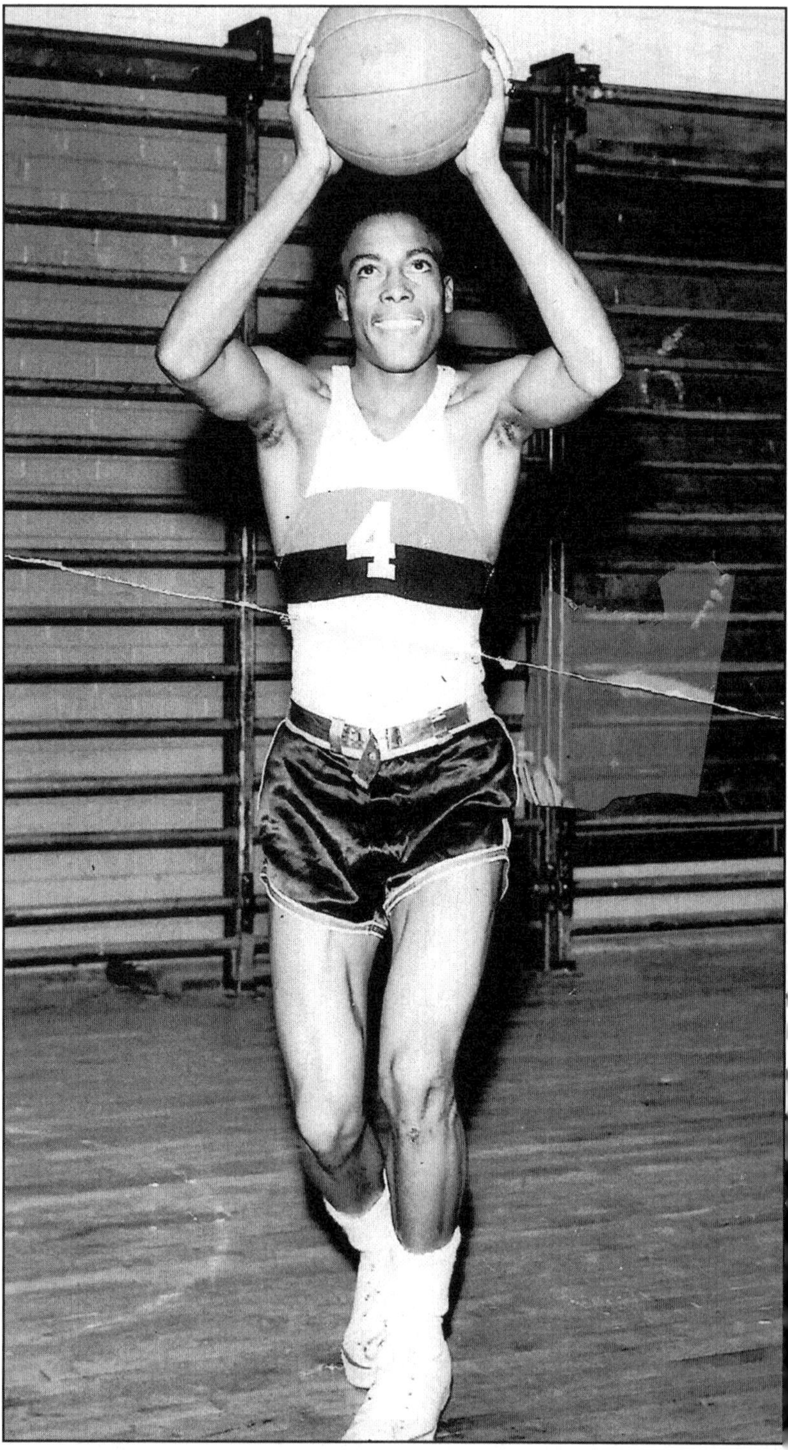

had North Philadelphia, which had Herb Janey and T. Parham. You had Ray Chinks Scott and myself as the fourth team. As we arranged those pick-up games, the guys would always say to me "Where we going to play tomorrow?" "What we going to do?" And I'd say, "We going to play at Moyland, 25th and Diamond." Or "We going to play at Haddington, 57th and Haverford." So then I got the idea, why don't we just take those sections of the city with the players and why don't we form teams? And after that, players like Wilt Chamberlain, Jay Norman, Guy Rodgers, also began to play. Then Woody Salsberry and Andy Johnson and others came to the city, so they played. That's how we formed the league

Here I also need to mention a gentleman by the name of Cal Smith, another important name. Cal Smith was a part of my life since I was probably fourteen years old. He was the second black in the city of Philadelphia to play on a white team. T. Parham and I used to ride with Cal Smith when he was playing for a team called the Norristown Blocks. He was such a big-time star when he was young, the Norristown Blocks would provide gas for him to get to the games. Well, he took T. and me under his wing. He was always there for me. He became my hero and my protector. They called him Rocky because he was a Marine that could knock people out. So he wouldn't let anybody bother me. He passed away about three years ago, but he was part of the building of the Baker League and the building of the Sonny Hill League.

Now what happened with the Sonny Hill League was that we had a group of youngsters who were the children of the people who played basketball. We had T. Parham's son, John Chaney's son, Herb Janey's son, my son and others. So I decided to form a little team that played before the Baker League games—a little entertainment piece. At that time, they were eight, nine years old, and they just became a crowd favorite. As they got older, I began to wonder what to do with them. So I decided to form The Sonny Hill League. That's how it started. From that, which was a five-team league, we have evolved over the past forty years into a league with over seventy teams.

Even when I was forming the league in 1968, though, it was never really about basketball. It was about helping young people. At that time, we had gang warfare in Philadelphia. And it was difficult for individuals to cross certain turfs. In West Philadelphia, people had to ask, "Can I go to South Philadelphia?" From South Philadelphia, "Can I go to North Philadelphia?" From North Philadelphia, "Can I go to West Philadelphia?" From there, "Can I go to Germantown?" What I found was that because of the reputation that I had built through the years, people knew Sonny Hill. So when I named my league "The Sonny Hill League," it wasn't about ego; it was about creating space for children to be able to move around the city like I had as a child. One of the things that gave me great pleasure initially was the fact that players in my league could travel across different sections of the city. If they were stopped by gangs along the way, the kids could say, "I'm going to play in the Sonny Hill League" and the gang members would say, "You can walk." That meant a lot to me.

It was from that experience, I began to understand how to infuse ideas about life beyond basketball into the league. It's great to be a basketball player. It's great to be an athlete. It's great to be an entertainer. It's great to be whatever you're doing in the present. But what are you going to do if it's taken away? And in sport, it will be taken away because you only have a short period of time to maximize your skills. After that, you got to get in the real world. That's when I began to infuse that philosophy of "reaching back" into the league. We began to work with our young people to make sure they understood "you're not just playing basketball. You also have to be pretty good in school." I brought in a gentleman by the name of Mr. Bill Jordan, who ran a tutoring program for over twenty-five years. Bill Jordan would come over to the games and, with some of those youngsters who didn't go to tutoring, he would take them right off the basketball floor. That sent a message to the whole league that you don't mess with what's going on. You better do what you need to do.

That is why "Education is your best shot" is on the shirt of every player in the Sonny Hill League because truly, if you're going to move ahead in our society, you need an education. People don't understand that we live in a capitalistic society that's about money. You get the money by getting an education. If you don't get an education, the likelihood of getting to the money is not that great. What I've found over the years, though, is that from an educational point of view, the United States has regressed, not progressed. We're going backwards. As we speak right now, the numbers are horrifying. We are seventy-six in the world in education. There are seventy-five countries that are before us. Fifty percent of our youngsters are dropping out of public school. Only fifty-two percent of the girls and forty-six of the boys are graduating. That doesn't mean they're graduating with the good academics, though. Sometimes the students are pushed through because the system has to push them through. We are even starting to fail at the college level. At one time the United States was number one in the world for college graduates. Now we're twelfth.

I have found, though, that you have to prepare for life after sports. Today youngsters can play basketball from maybe age six to maybe thirty-six years, but what are they going to do with for the next sixty years? I've seen too many situations where basketball players were outstanding in their period, but they didn't maximize it because they didn't understand the importance of education. Education gives you the opportunity to get to where you want to go over the long period. So we have to teach our young people the importance of education. And education is not just formal education. Education is also a worldly education. You could get an education by just keeping your mouth shut, ears and eyes open, absorbing and learning through that point of view. What better way to teach them these values than through something they enjoy? Whether it's basketball or art or something else that they take to?

Today, I tell people that I live in a time tunnel stopped at 1968—the year I formed the Sonny Hill League—because the league is the same today as it was back then. People ask, "How did you do that?" Well, the reason we were able to do that is we set the tone early. We hold them responsible. Sometimes it's the smallest thing, but it's about sending a message, setting a tone and they know it. So when the new people come in, the older players who've been in the program grab them when they step out of line and say, "Can't do that here." Therefore, the values are transmitted from the older group to the new group.

As a leader, you need to set the tone. I've always been a leader. From day one everything that I've been involved in—the 16th Street Cardinals, the Baker League, the Sonny Hill League—I've always been a leader. When I was young, I set the tone as a baseball and basketball player. Now that I'm older, I set the tone in how to deal with young people, using basketball as a vehicle for later life. But a leader, I think, leads by example. I don't think a leader accomplishes anything by being vocal or by standing on the sidelines saying, "I want this done," "You pick up this," and "You do all that." They take the lead from you. They have to see you working hard. So I've always done it differently. I do this or I do that *with their support*. I have not built this by myself. I've built this off the backs of all of them who have been with me over the years. They deserve as much as credit as I do, because without them I couldn't get it done.

So when I look back at my work, I get great pleasure that my emphasis on education and life after basketball was so important to the kids involved in the league. Almost every day, people from different backgrounds, different ethnicities, different parts of the city, different parts of the country stop me and they'll say, "I played in the league." They tell me how important the league was to them. They tell me how they're passing the values of the league on to their youngsters, and how their youngsters are passing it on to their friends. I just had one of my young guys, Greg Godfrey, come in to visit last week. I've known Greg Godfrey since he was like six years old. Greg and his brother ~~all~~ went to my basketball camp. They played in my league. I was invited to his wedding. I've become part of his family. Now he's expecting a child. He said to me, "Mr. Sonny, I can't wait till my boy gets here so he can play in the league." I said "He better start saying prayers for me. I'm seventy-three years old."

But I also have people who have fallen down. I have one player who went to West Philadelphia High School, played on that great West Philadelphia High School team, the one with Gene Banks. He's one year behind Gene, but he's on the West Philadelphia team. He had a chance to go play at Kentucky. Things didn't work out there, so he ended up playing basketball at Rutgers. Played ball overseas. But he fell down. Got involved in drugs, in negativity. His life was going nowhere. Then he got obese. Life was going nowhere. We stayed in contact. Whenever I saw him I tried to encourage him. He had great respect for me, still does. He just graduated from college. That's the kind of thing that happens all the time.

What I like most about it is that they respect me. I have young people coming into the program who really don't know my background. Whatever I did in basketball, nobody knows about that. They don't even know the long history of the Sonny Hill League. But they do know that this is a league that's been around for a period of time and, when they come in, they see the respect. They come by and they smile at me and want to speak to me. They want to walk up to me. They want to hug me. I'll ask them a question, like which school they've been at, do they get good grades. They say, "Yeah Mr. Sonny" and I'll say, "Well give me hug." Nobody gives them hugs. So I give them a hug and you can just feel how much they revere that. Next they go tell their friends, "I was talking to Mr. Sonny. Mr. Sonny gave me a hug." And then the others jump in line. So that's a great feeling.

This has been an amazing life, a Cinderella life. Every step along the way, I've been that kind of person to whom people gravitate and I've often asked myself why: Why did Dr. Leon Sullivan decide to take me under his wing? Was it so that I could play baseball and basketball? He had other people who played baseball and basketball, but I became one of his favorites. Why did Coach Wooley see something in me that I didn't see at that time when I was in high school? Why did Pete Gillespie see something in me and share something with me at that time? Why did Joe Ercolani establish a relationship with me when I was young, but maintain a relationship with me until he died? How did I end up getting a job at Teamsters Local 169 and having Frank Keane take me under his wing? Why did he mentor me and move me along in the labor industry where I was for thirty-four years and retired as secretary of the treasury? Why did the Pearsons, one of the big sporting goods people in this city for years, who ran the old industrial league, decide to take me under their wing? I think it was because of the way I conducted myself. They liked the way I walked, they liked the way I talked, they liked the way I dressed, they liked the way I carried myself—the lessons I learned as a child from my grandmother and great grandparents. All of that's important.

That's what I try to impress upon my young people. People judge you by two things, whether you realize it or not. The first thing they judge you by is how you look. How do you look visually? Do you have to be dressed like Sonny Hill? No. But you should look good. How do you speak? Do you have to speak like I'm speaking? No. I learned to speak like this over the years, but you need to know how to hold a conversation. Those are the two things that people judge you by right away. Right or wrong, they already summed you up and, at that point, it's hard to change whatever that first impression.

How do people perceive me? Perception is always from a distance. There are people who have a perception of who I am from a distance and then there are a minute few who really understand who I am. And the person that I am is the same person that the good Lord sent here seventy-three years ago. I never realized until five or ten years ago that I've been sent here by Him to do His work. As long as I do His work, He continues to reward me with all these earthly things. There's no other explanation that can be given for a guy who was born in 1936. Life expectancy for people born in 1936 was 59 ½. I am now 73 years old. Opportunities for people born in 1936, whether they were black or white, rich or poor, would never have enabled me to be a part of the things I've accomplished in my life so far and things that are still happening. So it's all about the blessing. It's all about the timing. The timing for me was 1936, July 22. All of these things that I've been able to do, I would not have been able to accomplish if it were not for being born on that day and Him giving me the blessing to do what He wants me to, which is to give back all of the things He's given me. Because, remember what I said before: I'm not a receiver, I'm a giver.

I'll start with my grandfather, Santos Amaro, who was a Hall of Fame baseball player in Cuba and Mexico. His nickname was El Canguro, the Kangaroo. He was a huge man, immense, 6'4", but very quiet. He had a quiet kind of strength. We would visit him when I was young. I remember every morning he would wake up, put on his hat, get dressed, shower, have breakfast and then leave real early in the morning for a walk. He would walk five, ten miles a day. Then in the middle of the day, he would come back and have lunch.

One of the stories my dad used to tell me was kind of a combination of my father and my grandfather. My grandfather was playing in Havana, Cuba, which at that time was the place to be. Cuba had these elaborate stadiums. My dad gets called to the major leagues for the St. Louis Cardinals, and, naturally, my dad tells his father, "Listen, I'm in the big leagues, please come visit." So my grandfather comes over to St. Louis and he walks into the locker room, and very, very quietly looks around, left and right, checks out all the facilities. Then he whispers into my dad's ear, "Is this the major league club?" It was just so vastly different from Cuba. He was amazed that there was such a huge difference between the two facilities in Havana and St. Louis. The major leagues were supposed to be the top dog, but Cuba had the way better facilities.

My grandfather left Cuba for Mexico when he met my grandmother. The Cuban national team, which he was on, was in some type of Pan-American games in Mexico. While there, he met my grandmother, who was the catcher on the Mexican women's team. They ended up getting married, having two kids and staying there. At the time, Mexico was one of the best places to play baseball for anybody of color. My dad used to tell stories all the time about some of the players who played in the Mexican league. There was a tremendous amount of talent there. My grandfather ended up being a player and a player manager. He became somewhat legendary there. Obviously he would have had a very good chance of being in the major leagues, but since he was someone of color, I mean he was completely dark-skinned, he didn't have the opportunity to play in the major leagues at that time. That was prior to Jackie Robinson.

Even after Jackie Robinson, there were all types of barriers and issues that colored players had to deal with on a daily basis in major league baseball. Discrimination didn't stop in certain areas of the country just because of Jackie Robinson. It just didn't. Ballplayers of color weren't allowed to participate in certain events, eat in certain restaurants, stay in certain hotels. That affected my dad, Rubén Amaro, Sr., very directly. When my dad came to the United States, he played at a variety of minor and major leagues levels, but he still faced discrimination. If the team would stop off at a bus stop and the players would go in and have dinner, he couldn't eat there if it was "no coloreds allowed." So there were times when they'd be travelling for 14 -15 hours, and the team would have to stop off for breakfast and he wouldn't be able to go in. The teams would protest, saying "We're not going to eat here; you're going to lose all this revenue if you don't let Rubén Amaro and some of the other players of color into the restaurant." My dad couldn't even stay at the team hotel in Clearwater during spring training, back when all the teams stayed in a team hotel. And again, the team protested and tried to stay at another place.

Sometimes there was even the threat of violence. I remember him telling me of one time when he was on a minor league team playing somewhere in Texas that was seriously prejudiced. My dad might have been the only player of color on the field. Well, somebody hit one of my dad's teammates with a pitch. The other team retaliated and "off they went." The teams got into a big brawl, which back then happened all the time. It wasn't a big deal. It was just part of the game. My dad started to rush onto the field, but the manager grabbed him and pushed him back into the clubhouse. He said, "Rubén, if you start fighting, these people in the stands are going come out there and lynch you." I mean it's very, very poignant to me that my dad had to go through such things. Coming through the minor leagues and trying to make his way through in a new country, learning a new language and all this stuff, and then having people tell him that he can't eat at this particular restaurant, can't sleep in a certain hotel, can't support his teammates. I can't even imagine it.

My dad was a very self-educated guy. Back then, the league didn't have the support programs that it does now for people from the Dominican Republic, Mexico and Venezuela. Today, the league helps them assimilate into society. For instance, there are English classes and other programs to make life easier for them. Now players are a little better prepared to be in a new country and make their way through baseball. They didn't have any of that back then. You had to basically do it yourself. And while my dad went to college and was educated, he basically taught himself English. He used to read a lot and watch a lot of TV. He loved movies. He loved to read. So he got a tremendous grasp of the vocabulary and learned English well. He still carries an accent, but with his vocabulary, he speaks as if he was born in the United States. I remember my mom and my dad sitting up in bed, giving each other language lessons. My dad would give my mom a vocabulary word in Spanish and she would tell him what it meant, then she would do the same with my dad. I grew to respect that effort. I started to understand that this must be really, really tough to all of a sudden be in this world where you're trying to make your way as an athlete and at the same time trying to figure out how to live in this new society.

One of the neatest stories that made me understand what my dad was all about, how he was viewed by the other players, occurred when Pete Rose was with the Phillies. My dad worked with Pete on ground balls every day and, for whatever reason, they had some kind of a bond there. Pete Rose didn't really have a whole lot of things in his locker, not a lot of family pictures. He used to hang his clothes, maybe hang up his batting gloves and dry them out. He was very baseball oriented. The one thing he did have was a baseball card of my dad. He put it right next to his name, just stuck it there. I was like, damn, you know, that's really, really cool. Pete Rose has one thing, one picture in his locker, and it's my dad.

It was in the 80's, when I was a batboy and my dad was a first base coach for the Phillies, that I decided baseball would be the thing to do. My dad had wanted me to play soccer in the worst way. He wanted to send me to camp in England because he thought I had potential. I had some success playing soccer, probably more success as a high school player in soccer than I did in baseball. But I think that spending the time with those Phillies teams in the early 80's as a bat boy, with the first two years being with my dad, were probably the biggest impetus behind me giving it a shot to play professional baseball.

I never really was in awe of professional baseball because I grew up in the game, but as I was with the team, I started to realize that some of the players on the Phillies were just incredible. I mean really, really good: Mike Schmidt, probably the team's best baseball player of all time; Steve Carlton, arguably the best left-handed pitcher of all time; Larry Bowa; Bob Boone; Greg Luzinski; and Gary Maddox. They were just some great players. Plus we were winning at the time. It was kind of the apex of that era. They had all these guys who were just coming through the farm system, and then all the sudden, this whole talent just burst into the glory days of the Phillies organization. I happened to be around and be a part of it. I think a lot of that snowballed into "Wow, it would be awesome to be a baseball player." So that probably had a lot to do with my decision to try to become a professional player.

Now when you come from the East Coast and you're a position player, unless you were born with amazing natural abilities—speed, power, an ability to hit—it doesn't really work for you. I mean it just doesn't happen. You're not going to end up being a major league player. I was one of those guys. I had a couple of assets. I could switch hit. I could run well. I had a couple of tools that were helpful, but I was limited. I didn't have the physical size. I was really very raw. But the one thing I did have was the mentality that I would never be outworked. So when I got the opportunity to come out to Stanford, which was one of the highest-ranking teams in the nation, I realized what the competition was like and that I would have to work very hard at baseball. So I just told myself, "Do as much as you can and work as hard as you possibly can to make the team." Ultimately, that hard work paid off for me. I ended up playing all four years there, becoming team captain my senior year, ultimately helping my team win the College World Series for the first time.

We were in the middle of the College World Series when they had the Major League Baseball draft. I remember hoping that I would be called the first day. My dad was there to watch us play, and he had heard from the other scouts that I was having a great year. Scouts were saying, "He's become a prospect" or "He probably won't get past the seventh." So I figured if I'm not going past the seventh, then I'll probably get drafted on the first day, but I didn't get called. I was bummed out. I figured I may not get drafted at all now. But then the phone rings in my hotel room. Jesse Flores, who drafted for the California Angels, says, "Is this Rubén?" "Yeah." Then he said, "We gotcha." I was the Angels tenth pick.

Back then when you were a rookie, you were a rookie. You were a peon. There was a respect factor. The Angels team that I played for had veterans like Dave Winfield, Dave Parker, Lance Parrish, Mark Langston and Chuck Finley. All of these studs. I remember sitting there going, "Oh my God." Even though I probably shouldn't have been in awe of them because of my father and grandfather's background, I still thought, "Oh my God, I can't believe I'm in the big leagues. I can't believe I'm lockered next to Dave Winfield and Dave Parker, two monstrous human beings who had been in the major leagues for so long." I remember my very first catch with a major league player was actually with Dave Winfield, and I'm thinking, "My God, here I am in the major leagues, you know, throwing with Dave Winfield." I couldn't even feel the ball. I made my first throw to him and I bounced it to him. I was like "I'm sorry, Dave!"

I was traded right after that season to Philadelphia. Now all of a sudden I'm in Philadelphia. I didn't have any expectations of making the team in spring training. I thought I was going to go to Triple-A. They needed an extra outfielder, though, and I had a fantastic spring and Jim Fregosi said, "You know, you're making this club." I'll never forget standing on the line when they introduce the opening day roster. I'm thinking to myself, "This is crazy!" Well, that was the opening day where Lenny Dykstra gets hit by a pitch. Now he's out. I'm the new centerfielder. Now I'm panicked because at that time, as a rookie, I'm thinking, "Oh my God, am I really ready for this?" My first two or three days, I just went off. I went nuts. I was leading the league in every category. I hit a home run and two doubles in my first game. Now everybody thought I was going to be the second coming of Joe DiMaggio. But after that first week I literally went in a tank. I started to think, "What am I doing here?" I ended up becoming my own worst enemy, putting a lot of pressure on myself to produce. The league started adjusting to me, but I didn't adjust back. So I just went into two huge slumps. It took me a while to get it going again.

Eventually, they had to weed me out and I got sent down briefly to the minor leagues, and then came back up, and finished off the year okay.

Now I never have enough great years in me to just say, "I made it." But when I was called back up the second time in '93, I actually began to feel like I was good enough to be a major league player. I don't have to go out there every day and worry about it. I knew that I was going to bounce around a lot, but I believed that I was good enough to play as a major league player. In fact, I remember reading the papers when I came back to the Phillies where they talked about the young players and the veteran players. They categorized me as one of the veterans. And I'm thinking to myself, "Really? I guess I am one of those." But by then I had already played in two World Series. Once you play in the World Series, not a whole lot of things awe you. I remember playing the World Series with Cleveland, being out there in right field at Fulton County Stadium in Atlanta, thinking to myself, "I cannot believe I'm in the World Series right now. This is so cool. I wasn't really that good of a player, but I worked hard, and I'm here. I'm playing in the World Series!"

My very last professional game was with the Phillies in Florida. It was already semi-official that I was going to be moving into the front office after the '98 season. I remember talking to my wife and family about making the transition. We talked about whether I should try to continue to be the 25th man on the team every year, for the next four or five years, or move to the front office. Physically I was in decent shape. I wasn't worn down, but I was aware how this opportunity to go from the field to the front office might not come again. I remember one key moment in making that decision, a conversation with my dad when I got my first "call up." I was in the Angels minor league system at the time and the manager told me I was going to the major leagues. I remember getting on the phone with my dad, crying, saying to him, "Dad, I'm going to the big leagues." And he said, "Son, I'm so proud of you. Now try to figure out a way to stay there. 'Cause getting there is one thing, staying there is another." And I said "Yeah, you're right." And then eight days later I'm back down in the minor leagues. So based on that conversation, I just said, "You know what? I'd be so stupid not to take this opportunity."

Since then, I've tried to bring my personal and professional experiences to the front office. I truly believe in diversity. I believe in it wholeheartedly. I believe in different cultural views. I believe in different people bringing different ideas and thought processes from different backgrounds to the table. I believe it's true in the major leagues that you have to have a mix of certain skills obviously, but also a mix of heart and desire. I really believe that works. One of the benefits of being on great teams and really, really bad teams is that I could see what really works and what doesn't. Obviously talent is important and at the end of the day you have to have the talent to have success. But it's also about putting together the pieces, both culturally and physically, that will work for us. I think it's really important to have diversity on the team. And we are very fortunate that we are in a system right now where the talent is equal to the kind of people that we want on our field. So if you look on our field right now, Jimmy Rollins, African American; Ryan Howard, African American; Carlos Ruiz, Latin American; Chase Utley, Caucasian; Raul Ibañez, Latin American; Shane Victorino, Hawaiian. You are looking at a diverse group of backgrounds that all happen to fit together because they're all pretty good people. Those beliefs have been very successful for us.

I remember riding on the float after the Phillies won the World Series in 2008 and looking around at the city, just watching and keying in on certain people. I could see 50, 60, 70-year-old men bawling, crying. I'm thinking to myself, "This guy can die and go to Heaven, and it won't matter now." We hadn't had such a positive feeling since 1993, which was a pinnacle year every fan could identify with. The '93 team was a fortunate group of players brought together somewhat by luck. It wasn't like they built the team. It was more like each player had his career year *that* year. I mean they literally had twenty-five people who had their best career years almost to a man. And it just happened to work out, and the fans identified with it. It was just huge, huge for the city. Then we had the strike. It went from being this euphoria to "screw baseball." Then the Phillies never rebuilt. The teams were just terrible. I mean I was on the teams. We were terrible. It took us a long time to get back going the other way. I've been on that roller coaster, I've been through the whole gambit. For us to get back to the pinnacle again was amazing, it was really amazing.

Really fortunate.

CARLOS RUIZ

"I knew that with one more pitch, we were the World Champions"

One of my dreams as a child was that I wanted to be a professional baseball player and play in the World Series. I grew up in David Chiriqui, Panama. It was not a poor neighborhood, but it wasn't the richest, either. There you have the essentials around you: a clinic, a small school and a ballpark. Growing up playing baseball in Panama is very different than playing in America, though. Here it is more organized. There are more facilities and resources. In Panama they don't have all that organization, though it has improved a lot.

I'm the only one in my family who liked baseball. My family is a very big, very united family. There are nine brothers and sisters from my mom's side, and I have three brothers in my immediate family. I was the only one who practiced sports, though. I used to practice baseball, football or soccer. I also liked to play volleyball. I got that from my mom because she practiced volleyball all the time.

But baseball has always been my favorite sport.

I remember when I was sixteen playing baseball, there were scouts watching me. My position wasn't catcher back then; I was an infielder but because of my size it was quite a challenge to play infield. The scouts told me that more than likely it would not happen for me as an infielder, that I wouldn't become a professional player. I needed more abilities, like running, in order for that to happen. In my heart, though, I felt that I was going to find that opportunity some way.

So I continued playing, representing my province and doing it quite well. I still wasn't catching. I was continuing to play the infield. Finally the opportunity came for me to play my position of choice—catcher. In Panama, there was a Phillies scout looking for talent who worked for the Phillies. He told me to go ahead and play catcher and they may sign me. Well, the Phillies did sign me and they sent me

Uno de mis sueños como niño era que yo quería ser un jugador profesional de béisbol y jugar en la Serie Mundial. Yo me crié en David Chiriquí, Panamá. No era un barrio pobre, pero tampoco era el más rico. Allí hay lo esencial a tu alrededor: el centro de salud, una pequeña escuela, y un parque de béisbol. Sin embargo, jugando béisbol en Panamá mientras uno es muy joven es muy diferente que jugando en América durante el mismo period de tiempo. En los Estados Unidos es más organizado. Hay más facilidades y recursos. En Panamá no tienen todas esa organización, aunque ha mejorado mucho.

Soy el único en mi familia que me gustaba el béisbol. Mi familia es muy grande, una familia muy unidad. Hay nueve hermanos y hermanas de parte de mi mamá, y tengo tres hermanos en mi familia inmediata. A pesar de tener una familia tan grande yo fui el único que practicaba deportes. Yo practicaba béisbol y fútbol. También me gustaba jugar volibol. Obtuve ese interese por parte de mi mamá porque ella practicaba volibol todo el tiempo.

Pero béisbol siempre ha sido mi deporte favorito.

Yo recuerdo cuando tenía dieciséis y jugaba béisbol, habían scouts observando. Mi posición en ese entonces no era receptor, era el infield y debido a mi tamaño era un reto. Los scouts me dijeron que lo más probable no iba a ocurrir para mí como un infielder, que no me voy a convertir en un jugador professional. Según ellos, yo necesitaba más habilidades para lograr eso, como correr más rápido. En mi corazón, sin embargo, sentí que iba a encontrar esa oportunidad de alguna manera.

Así yo continue jugando, representando my provincia y sobresaliendo. Todavía no estaba jugando la posición de receptor. Continue jugando el infield. Finalmente, la oportunidad se presento para jugar mi posición ideal, receptor. En Panamá habia un scout que trabaja para los Phillies y él estaba buscando talento. Él me dijo que continue jugando la posición de receptor

to the Dominican Republic (DR). I will always remember my first professional experience with the Phillies DR team. I made a promise to my teammates that if we won the championship there, I would cut my hair. We won and I had to do it. I was there for a year, then the Phillies sent me to the U.S. It was a great experience knowing that I was in the place that I wanted to be.

Adjusting to the culture was quite an experience. While I spoke a little English, the team had a great system of English classes in the minor leagues for me to learn more. Also, from being around the ball players, I have learned about the culture. But it was those classes that they offered in the morning that made my transition easier. Making the Reading Phillies was a challenge, but I was ready for the fight. That's something that I will always remember—battling for a roster spot.

Playing in the World Series was something very special to me. I will always cherish catching the final ball in the World Series. I waited with a lot of anxiety. I knew that with one more pitch, we were the World Champions and what would happen after would be incredible. Even today, when I see all of the stories and the videos about the World Series, it brings a certain level of emotion. I can't explain to you how it feels. I know that it is something that will always be in my heart, something that will give me more desire to work. To me it is something very special and something that I will remember for the rest of my life as if it was yesterday.

For years, my family was only able to watch me play here in Philadelphia on TV. This year for the first time they watched me at a stadium. I was a little bit nervous because it was the first time that my mom watched me as a professional. She was emotional as well. It is hard to put into words, but it's very exciting to know that your family and thousands of fans alongside them are watching you.

It has been quite a journey from Panama to where I am today. What advice would I give to someone who is trying to be where I am? The most important thing is to get a good education. With education and hard work, you can reach every goal that you set.

y que quizas me van a firmar. Así, los Phillies me firmaron y me enviaron a la República Dominicana. Siempre recordere mi primera experiencia professional con el equipo de los Phillies en la República Dominica. Le hice una promesa a mi compañeros de equipo que si ganabamos el campeonato, yo me cultaría mi cabello. Ganamos, y tuve que hacerlo. Yo me demore ahi por un año, entonces los Phillies me environ a los Estados Unidos. Fue una gran logro cuando yo llegue al sitio donde queria llegar.

Adaptación a la cultura fue toda una experiencia. Mientras yo hablaba algo de inglés, el equipo tenía un gran sistema de clases de inglés en las ligas menores para poder aprender más. También, pasando el tiempo con los jugadores, he aprendido acerca de la cultura. Pero fueron esas clases que ofrecieron en la mañana que hicieron mi transición más fácil.

Eso dicho, logrando hacer parte del equipo de los Reading Phillies fue un reto, pero yo estaba listo para la lucha. Eso es algo que siempre recordaré - luchando para ser parte del equipo.

Jugando en la Serie Mundial fue una cosa muy especial para mi. Siempre voy a apreciar en coger la pelota final en la Serie Mundial. Yo la esperé con gran ansiedad. Yo sabía que estabamos a ley de un lanzamiento para ser los campeones mundiales y que lo que ocurriría a partir de ahí sería increíble. A propósito, hoy cuando veo todas las historias y videos sobre la Serie Mundial, trae un cierto nivel de emociones. No puedo explicarte a ti como uno se siente. Se que es algo que siempre va estar en mi corazón. Algo que me va a dar mas deseo de trabajar. Para mi es algo muy especial y algo que recordaré durante toda mi vida como si hubiese sido ayer.

Por varios años, mi familia solamente podían verme jugar en Philadelphia por televisión. Este año por primera vez, me vieron en un estadio. Yo estaba un poco nervioso porque fue la primera vez que mi mamá me vio jugar como un profesional. Ella también estaba muy emocional. Es difícil describer la emoción en palabras, pero es muy emocionante saber que tu familia, junto a miles de otros fans, está viéndote jugar.

Ha sido un viaje desde Panamá a donde estoy hoy. ¿Qué consejos le daría a un joven que está tratando de llegar a donde yo estoy? Lo primero es recibir una buena educación. Con la educación y el trabajo duro tu puedes alcanzar todos los metas que tu has determinado.

Ball

LARRY COLANGELO, JR

"But that tightness with the fans, that's when it was real, that's when the fans were a part of the team. When Russia wouldn't come out to the second period because they were afraid we were too rough. Yeah, it was about the players, but I don't think the players would have hit it as hard if the fans weren't behind them. It's easy to play when you know it's 20,000 against five, you know what I mean?"

To this day, I still remember that the first sports jersey I ever had was Philadelphia Flyers Peter Zezel, number 25.

He wasn't a star, but he was my guy. Maybe it had to do with my birthday being on the 25th. Maybe it had to do with the fact that my uncle and godfather, Mark Colangelo, who has done the ice for the Flyers for a long time, got the jersey for me. Not many people had a Zezel jersey back then.

My uncle would take me to Flyers games all the time. We would get these three seats in the lower level of the Spectrum, the last row right behind Ron Hextall. After the game, he would bring me over to met Rick Tocchet and Ron Hextall. He knew all the guys, all the Gretzkys, all the legends. My uncle even played amateur hockey for a while. One of the coolest things is about five years ago, there was an open hockey rink, and we ended up playing together on the same ice. Full gear, full pads, line changes. It was cool to play with your uncle, the person who took you under his wing. He was my hockey influence.

I don't know how my brother ended up being a bigger hockey fan than me, but my dad definitely had that relationship with my little brother—they bonded over hockey. About five years ago, my dad and brother got season tickets. Just as I moved out of the house, they're like, "Let's go for it." They started with two seats up in the 200 level, and we would all trade-off on who was going to go to each game. We'd go to town. There was an excitement about getting ready to go: "What jersey are you going to wear?" "Dad I've got a t-shirt 'cause you don't have one." It's that whole forty-five minutes before you get in the car thing, especially when the playoffs begin; nothing beats playoff hockey.

I liked being in the upper level with them more than the lower level by the goalie. It's just madness up there. It's a rowdier crowd. You get excited. You turn around and yell at people "to get up" and they do—that camaraderie aspect of Philly. That's the coolest thing. That's the attitude that team had with their fans. I mean obviously I wasn't born when the Flyers played the Russians. But that tightness with the fans, that's when it was real, that's when the fans were a part of the team. When Russia wouldn't come out for the second period because they were afraid we were too rough. Yeah, it was about the players, but I don't think the players would have hit it as hard if the fans weren't behind them. It's easy to play when you know it's 20,000 against five, you know what I mean?

Maybe that's my dream world of what it would be like to be an athlete. I'm hearing that music in my heart, singing that National Anthem. I'm waiting in that tunnel and the metal music is playing. I skate out and that stadium is glowing orange and everyone is losing their minds. For me, if I'm in that moment, I don't care who you are, you could be Wayne Gretzky and you're not touching me. If 20,000 people are screaming for me, you have no chance. You actually have no chance. That's what the stadium has turned into. You feel it in the stands.

Until 2008, I'd never seen one of our teams win a championship. Ever. You know we lost two Stanley Cup finals. We lost in the Super Bowl. I'm not a big basketball fan, but we got whupped by the Lakers. I can remember 1993 with the Phillies. I was 12 years old, laying on the floor when Joe Carter hit that home run that beat us in the World Series. 2008 changed everything.

I mean, the World Series for me, I could go on forever. I'll never be able to explain how awesome it was that night. That's definitely my best sports memory. Me, my mom, my dad, my bro and sister. All five of us. We've got the tickets and my sister's got the little stupid finger on—she always wanted one of them. She never got it until she was 23. Just little stupid things like that I remember. Just walking up to the stadium and realizing, again obviously it was mixed feelings, but you kind of felt it was coming. The series was 3-1 at this point. Walking into the stadium, you see the band playing and you see the Phillies at the back of stadium. We were actually at the World Series. We were playing for a championship. I think that was a little more important for me than for my brother and sister. I may be a little arrogant to say that, but I've been waiting. And I know I'm not the biggest baseball fan that I could be, but I love the Phillies, and I've been waiting 25 years for this day.

So we finally get there and it starts pouring.

Cole Hamels is striking people out, but it keeps getting muddier and we're freezing to death. We put our ponchos on, and we're sitting there. I waited 25 years for this, and now it's raining. My mom's wearing a trash bag at this point. We go underneath the roof and they say, "This game will be postponed." And it was just all that frustration coming back to the fans 'cause they had to wait one more day. And everyone, you know, used very bad language. It was the night! We were winning. That was supposed to be the night we waited 25 years for. You could see the disappointment in everybody's face. It was right back to that same old Philly attitude—"No matter what, they'll always rip our hearts out." I had to drive back to New York the next day, and I'm calling in to my family, "Are they going to play? Are they going to play?" I got to leave work early. It's a couple hours drive, and I've got to get there before the game. And they don't know, and there's tension the whole day—will tonight be the night?

Then I woke up to sunshine in New York, and I knew today was the day. This is it. They can't put this off another day. I got my bottle of champagne in New York before I went to work. Drive down to Philadelphia and the five of us walk up to the stadium. The band's playing and people are waving flags—just like a few days before. They didn't even have to play the three innings. They did not even have to play. You felt it. You knew it was the night. You knew it was the night you were waiting for your entire life. And with every out, the entire stadium yelled how many more outs were left.

Little things that night will always stick out to me. We're sitting there right before the game starts, and the guy sitting behind us was with his 11 year-old boy. The dad went to get him pizza, and I'm talking to the little kid. He doesn't understand what's going on, but he's holding a baseball. And I was like where'd you get this? He tells me Cole Hamels gave it to him before the game. He didn't know it then, but he's going to look back at that night for the rest of his life.

I still get emotional thinking about it. I'm getting all emotional now, but it was just... I didn't even see the final pitch. As soon as that ball went by, as soon as Lidge threw the last pitch—strike out, ballgame, he dropped to his knees, I didn't see anything after that. And I just picked up my brother, I'm holding him up, and I'm crying, everybody's crying and finally...it finally happened.

So we just walked out, grabbed the champagne from the car, popped it and it was just, you know, people who I don't even know, we've got like thirty-forty pictures of us; me and some random guy; my brother and my mom with some crazy guy with a big Cole Hamels life size thing. And I'm hugging people and picking them up—just things that don't usually happen. This guy we probably wouldn't even make eye contact with usually, because that's just how it is, but it was like everyone was your best friend, everyone was your brother, people jumping on each other's shoulders, people driving down Broad Street yelling, "Hop on my car. I'll give you a ride up to City Hall!" That was definitely the coolest thing in my life, by far.

I probably played *We Are the Champions* on my ipod for three days afterwards, freaking out the entire time. You've been hearing that song in Disney movies, in *Any Given Sunday*. You've been watching every other team take that walk. Just singing it in the stadium and, finally, like, it's actually true. It didn't make sense. And driving back to work, you know, it was just cloud 9. Totally cloud 9.

VANESSA RODRIGUEZ

"Rained Out at the Ballgame"

It all started at a baseball game, just me and my dad. I couldn't wait for this day. Not because it was my first game, because I really didn't care about the game. But because I was going to spend some time with the only man I ever really cared about. He was a stern, typical traditional Mexican father who really never showed any type of affection towards me.

As soon as we arrived at the Phillies stadium, I felt a rush of nerves and excitement build up in my stomach. As we sat down in our seats the game started. Then the best thing ever happened—drops of cold water fell on my cheek. Thunder crashed and the tarp was rolled out. The game was delayed.

The next thing I knew, my dad and I were talking like never before. Usually when we talked, we talked about the bad things I would do—like getting bad grades or staying up late. But this time it was different. We talked about me and guys, about him not letting me have a lot of liberty because he was scared of letting me go. About how he came to this country so I could have a better future. Things we didn't know about each other, things that connected us in a special way like no other. I felt like a little girl who had just learned how to speak, a little girl who could not stop talking.

The baseball players were all positioned. The drops had stopped and so did me and my dad. And I suddenly stared at my dad. Then my father asked me if everything was fine. I said, "Yeah, Papi. You know something? I love you." He responded, "I love you to, mi'ja."

From that moment, I knew my father really loved me. Despite the fact that I'm one out of three sisters, despite the fact that we really never connected before, nobody can ever take away that day and those five words my father said to me: "I love you too, mi'ja."

ABOUT THE EDITORS

Eliot Shorr-Parks, a graduate of Temple University, is Associate Editor of New City Community Press. *More Than a Game* is his first book. He is currently working on a project focused on Philadelphia football. You can read his coverage of Eagles football on BuzzonBroad.com. He is a life-long Philadelphia resident.

Steve Parks is an Associate Professor of Writing at Syracuse University and founder of New City Community Press (newcitycommunitypress.com). His previous books include *Gravyland: Writing Beyond the Curriculum in the City of Brotherly Love* and *Class Politics: The Movement for a Students' Right To Their Own Language*. He lives in Philadelphia with his family.